It's Still Greek to Me

Other Books by the Author

Using New Testament Greek in Ministry
Learn to Read New Testament Greek
New Testament Textual Criticism
Linguistics for Students of New Testament Greek
Linguistics and New Testament Interpretation (editor)
New Testament Criticism and Interpretation (editor, with David
    Dockery)

It's Still Greek to Me

An Easy-to-Understand Guide to Intermediate Greek

David Alan Black

BakerBooks

A Division of Baker Book House Co
Grand Rapids, Michigan 49516

© 1998 by David Alan Black

Published by Baker Books
a division of Baker Publishing Group
P.O. Box 6287, Grand Rapids, MI 49516-6287
www.bakerbooks.com

Eighth printing, November 2006

Printed in the United States of America

Library of Congress Cataloging-in-Publication Data
Black, David Alan, 1952–
    It's still Greek to me : an easy-to-understand guide to intermediate Greek / David Alan Black.
        p.   cm.
    Includes index.
    ISBN 10: 0-8010-2181-2
    ISBN 978-0-8010-2181-7
    1. Greek language, Biblical—Grammar. 2. Bible. N.T.—Language, style. I. Title.
PA817.B545   1998
487′.4—dc21   98-7826

To My Greek Students

Contents

PART 1: Up the Greek without a Paddle: *This Thing Called Grammar*

The Parts of Speech
NOUNS • ADJECTIVES • PRO-
NOUNS • VERBS • ADVERBS,
PARTICIPLES, PREPOSITIONS,
CONJUNCTIONS, INTERJECTIONS
Organizing the Greek Parts of Speech

A Word about Words
Conclusion
For Practice
Key Terms

The Sentence: Subject and Predicate
Types of Verbs
Modifiers
Classes of Sentences
Phrases
PREPOSITIONAL PHRASES •
VERBAL PHRASES

Clauses
NOUN CLAUSES • ADJECTIVAL
CLAUSES • ADVERBIAL CLAUSES
How to Analyze a Sentence
Conclusion
For Practice
Key Terms

PART 2: The Greeks Had a Word for It: *The Greek Noun System*

Preface

People who teach or write about Greek grammar tend to treat the subject as though it were a green vegetable: you may not like grammar, but it's good for you. The reason it's good for you, of course, is that the depth of your preaching or teaching from the New Testament depends in large part on how well you handle the original Greek. As a friend once put it, "A good preacher is like an iceberg: you see only 10 percent, but underneath you sense the other 90 percent." What he meant was that the key to effective preaching is the ability to simplify without becoming simplistic. Only a solid understanding of New Testament Greek grammar can give you this ability, and motivating you to continue your Greek studies is one of the main purposes of this book, even if grammar is not your cup of tea.

But enough lecturing. I learned very quickly when I first began teaching Greek more than twenty years ago that you don't have to do much sermonizing about the importance of Greek grammar to people whose livelihoods depend in large part on how well they communicate the Word of God. And I don't think it's necessary to do much preaching in the introduction to this book. The fact that you either have bought or are thinking about buying this book suggests that you do not need to be sold on the idea of becoming more conversant with Greek grammar. What you need to know is whether *It's Still Greek to Me* offers you something you can't get from the scores of other grammar books now on the market. I think it does.

It's Still Greek to Me evolved out of a series of Greek courses I have taught to many hundreds of students in colleges and seminaries in the United States, Germany, Korea, and India. In these courses my objective is to teach people how to use Greek effectively in their personal lives and ministries. What makes these courses different, however, is the approach. I don't think it's a good policy to make adults feel as if they're back in third grade, and so I go out of my way to make sure the topics I cover are relevant to adults, in particular to adults whose business is the ministry of the Word of God. I also go out of my way to present the principles of grammar in a manner that is lively, challenging, and even fun.

11

What I have tried to do—and think I have done—in *It's Still Greek to Me* is to write a guide to grammar that does more than simply rehash the same litany of "rules" and "principles" that have been talked about, written about, argued about, and sweated over for centuries. I have tried to organize the book in a manner geared to the way people actually *use* the language, and I have done my utmost to make this book not only accurate but easy to understand and enjoyable to read. I have tried, in short, to produce a true *user's* guide to New Testament Greek for the twenty-first century. The only prerequisites on your part are a basic knowledge of Greek—and a healthy sense of humor.

Having said all this, let me point out quickly that neither this book nor any of the courses on which it is based are meant to be the definitive work on Greek grammar and usage. Greek grammar is a huge, sprawling subject, and if you were so inclined, you could devote the better part of your life to studying a tiny segment of it—the participle, let's say. On the reasonably safe assumption that you are not so inclined, I have focused my attention in this book on those specific grammar and usage issues that are the most relevant to everyday Bible study and sermon preparation—and, just as importantly, on those misconceptions of grammar that can really hurt your preaching and teaching.

Each of the following chapters tells you something about the nuts and bolts of Greek grammar, how the pieces may be put together and taken apart again, and to what ends. I have put more emphasis in this book on *what* you should do if you want to use Greek effectively in your ministry and less on *why* it is grammatically incumbent upon you to do so. Yes, many of the guidelines in this book are supported by explanations that involve a grammatical principle. But whenever I have felt the need to clarify a grammatical guideline, I have done my best to keep the explanation brief and to the point—"less is more" being a fundamental law of writing as well as of teaching and public speaking.

In any event, if this book does nothing else, it will give you a better understanding of those grammar and usage standards that most ministers and educated lay people can be expected to subscribe to in the twenty-first century, and it will give you the knowledge and the understanding you need to incorporate those standards into your own ministry. For this reason alone, I think you will find *It's Still Greek to Me* a valuable book.

So, if you've ever had to admit "It's *still* Greek to me!" when asked about some point of Greek grammar, then this book is for you. As you brush up on your Greek, you will not only reacquaint yourself with the enduring significance of the Greek New Testament but also rediscover the indispensable role Greek plays in interpretation and preaching. Once that knowledge is part of your consciousness, I am sure you will find the language of the New Testament a circus ring of excitement as long as you live.

A Word to the Teacher

This book offers you and your students a succinct explanation of the most important grammatical constructions and categories of New Testament Greek. As such, it can be used as a textbook for direct instruction. It is intended primarily for those who have finished one year of instruction in Greek, and is thus best suited for the first half of second-year Greek. Its fourteen chapters can easily be covered in a one-semester course, with ample time for review and testing. Once the contents of this book have been digested, students should be encouraged to acquire an advanced reference grammar of New Testament Greek as well as other necessary study tools. I have made recommendations along these lines in the postscript.

It is hoped that students who have worked carefully through this book will be able to read the Greek New Testament with greater facility. The words used in the translation exercises are those that occur frequently in the New Testament, and many sentences are taken verbatim from the Greek New Testament. However, no Greek-to-English dictionary is included at the back of the book, and the references of the Bible passages in the exercises are, for the most part, not given. This prevents students from relying too heavily on their Greek text (or their English translations) and forces them to become acquainted with the basic tools of New Testament exegesis. (Obviously, students should be discouraged from consulting the answer key until *after* they have completed their own translations.)

No special instruction is given here in the areas of linguistics (including discourse analysis), exegesis, or textual criticism. These essential matters have already been treated in my other Baker volumes, *Linguistics for Students of New Testament Greek, Using New Testament Greek in Ministry*, and *New Testament Textual Criticism*. These books also have an intentional light touch and may profitably be used alongside the present volume in a second-year class.

To those teachers who elect to use *It's Still Greek to Me* as a text, I offer my thanks and invite comments and suggestions about any aspect of this book that may benefit future readers on either side of the desk.

Acknowledgments

Though I never planned it this way, most of my books have dealt in some way with New Testament Greek, despite the fact that I have always considered myself more a student of the language than an expert. I empathize with the author who complained to a critic, "I have written ten books, and each grows worse than the one before." "Not at all," rejoined the critic, "it is simply that your taste is improving."

Though my literary taste may have improved through the years, I remain painfully aware of the shortcomings in this book. It would have been a far less adequate volume, however, had it not been for the help of a supporting cast of mentors and guides. These include the late Dr. Harry Sturz of Biola University, under whom I began my Greek studies and with whom I had the privilege of working for several wonderful years before his untimely death; the late Professor Bo Reicke of the University of Basel, who made his hapless doctoral students undergo oral exams in both Greek and Latin and who constantly prodded us to read the text with that rarest of all scholarly attainments, common sense; Dr. Bernhard Wyss, professor emeritus of Greek philology at the same university, whose expertise in Greek grammar made a lasting and positive impression on me; Jim Weaver and Wells Turner, my exceedingly capable editors at Baker Books; and finally the countless number of Greek students I have had the honor of serving in a wide variety of settings through the years.

To these students, and to their successors, this book is dedicated with love and affection. I hope that all of you will emerge from reading it aglow in head and heart, fresh from a honeymoon with the Greek language, and that your reading and study of the Greek New Testament will be ever more enjoyable for you in the years ahead.

Abbreviations

BDF   F. Blass and A. Debrunner, *A Greek Grammar of the New Testament and Other Early Christian Literature*, trans. Robert W. Funk (Chicago: University of Chicago Press, 1961)

Dana and
Mantey   H. E. Dana and Julius R. Mantey, *A Manual Grammar of the Greek New Testament* (New York: Macmillan, 1957)

Robertson   A. T. Robertson, *A Grammar of the Greek New Testament in the Light of Historical Research* (Nashville: Broadman, 1934)

Wallace   Daniel B. Wallace, *Greek Grammar beyond the Basics: An Exegetical Syntax of the New Testament* (Grand Rapids: Zondervan, 1996)

Zerwick   Maximilian Zerwick, *Biblical Greek: Illustrated by Examples*, trans. Joseph Smith (Rome: Scripta Pontificii Instituti Biblici, 1963)

Cross-references to these sources are by page number.

PART 1

Up the Greek without a Paddle

This Thing Called Grammar

1

There's No Place like Rome

The Parts of Speech and Their Function

If you were an architect, you wouldn't talk about a building you've designed without mentioning its parts—bricks, girders, glass, and so on. In much the same way, grammarians discuss sentences in terms of their parts and the functions of those parts.

Both the grammarian and the architect find it convenient to use a specialized vocabulary in discussing their subjects. Architects speak of *joists* and *bearing walls*; grammarians speak of *verbs* and *participles*—the language of grammar.

When I lead workshops on grammar, people invariably ask me where they can find a comprehensive, simple guide to the terminology of grammar. Consider the first two chapters of this book as such a guide. Here you'll find the basic definitions, principles, and examples that anyone must understand to be grammatically informed.

Some readers may ask, "Do I need to know all these technical terms?" Let me answer this way: how would you like to have your car serviced by this team of mechanics?

"Think we ought to check this whatchamacallit?"
"No, that doodad over there seems to be the problem."
"Okay, hand me that thingamabob."
"The what?"
"You know, the doohickey."
"This?"
"No, the gizmo underneath it!"

Yes, you need to know the terms in chapters 1 and 2. The remainder of this book builds on these foundational concepts.

The Parts of Speech

The parts of speech are the pieces you use to put sentences and paragraphs together. To put them together properly, you need to know what each piece is called and what role it plays.

For centuries, words have been put into eight different categories, depending on the role they play in sentences. These categories are all derived from Latin, a language that provides an incredible portion of our minimum daily requirement of grammatical vocabulary. The Latin grammarians, of course, borrowed freely from the Greeks, but that was how the Romans operated in those days. (Greek and Latin share the same Indo-European origin and have a great deal in common.) The upshot was a general agreement on the following parts of speech:

- nomen (noun)
- pronomen (pronoun)
- verbum (verb)
- adverbium (adverb)
- participium (participle)
- praepositio (preposition)
- conjunctio (conjunction)
- interjectio (interjection)

All but the last of these were lifted virtually in mint condition from the Greeks, and English, perhaps the most notorious language borrower of all time, has followed suit by lifting them all. A quick look at the kinds of words that belonged to each category may be helpful.

Nouns

Nomen originally meant "name." A word was considered a *nomen* if it "named" a substance or quality. Thus, *book, house, truth,* and *wise* would all have belonged to the class *nomen.* Some members of the *nomen* family could be used to describe other members. A *nomen* that was used to describe another was called a *nomen adjectivum,* which means, roughly, "an assistant *nomen.*" Thus, in the sentence "she's a wise person," *wise* and *person* would each have been considered a *nomen. Wise* would have been a *nomen adjectivum,* while *person* would have been a run-of-the-mill *nomen.* Today we would classify *wise* as an adjective, and *person* as a noun. Any part of speech that functions as a noun is called a **substantive.**

One reason the early grammarians classed nouns and adjectives together was to avoid the question of what to call an adjective that is used as a noun (as in "a word to *the wise* is sufficient"). Besides, all the members of the *nomen* class had the same structure. Each could be seen as a sequence of two elements: a **stem** followed by an **ending.** The stem carried the basic meaning of the word, while the ending told you whether the word was singular or plural and gave you some idea of what the word was doing in the sentence. English still bears a faint resemblance to this Indo-European trait in such words as *dog, dogs, dog's,* and *dogs'.*

In Greek there were five different kinds of endings that all members of the *nomen* class carried around with them. (Latin nouns had six sets of endings.) These different kinds of endings are called **cases,** and they are: nominative, vocative, genitive, dative, and accusative.

- Nouns appeared in the **nominative case** chiefly when they were the subject of the verb. In the sentence "Sam works for me," *Sam* would appear in the nominative case.
- In the sentence, "Sam, you're fired," *Sam* would appear in the **vocative case**.
- The **genitive case** was frequently used to express possession. In the sentence "Sam's friends were not surprised," *Sam's* would be in the genitive case.
- A noun appears in the **dative case** when it is an indirect object. In the sentence "I gave Sam his severance pay," *Sam* would be in the dative case.
- Finally, direct objects appeared in the **accusative case**, as in "I still like Sam," where *Sam* would be in the accusative case.

Three more things need to be said about nouns. First, each noun in Greek and Latin belonged to one of three **genders: masculine, feminine**, or **neuter** (the term neuter simply means "neither" in Latin). If you're not used to it, this matter of gender can be a bit discomfiting. In his famous essay "The Awful German Language," Mark Twain spoofs the confusion produced by German gender by translating literally a conversation in a German Sunday-school book:

Gretchen: Wilhelm, where is the turnip?
Wilhelm: She has gone to the kitchen.
Gretchen: Where is the accomplished and beautiful English maiden?
Wilhelm: It has gone to the opera.

To Germans, of course, all of this makes perfectly good sense. They know that a tree is masculine, its buds are feminine, its leaves are neuter; that horses are sexless, clocks are feminine, and tables are masculine. Greek works in exactly the same way: it, too, has grammatical gender—*time* is masculine, *day* is feminine, and *year* is neuter. But keep in mind that the vast majority of nouns are not put in these three classes because there is something masculine, feminine, or neuter about them.

The ending of a Greek noun is often a guide to its gender, but gender must usually be learned by observation. In general, the names of winds, rivers, and months are masculine; the names of countries, islands, towns, trees, and abstract nouns (like *truth* or *love*) are feminine; and the names of fruits are neuter. Some nouns may be either masculine or feminine (e.g., ὁ θεός is *god,* but ἡ θεός is *goddess*). These nouns are said to be of **common gender**.

In addition to asking about the gender of a noun, you also have to ask which **declension** the noun belongs to. A declension, of which there are three in Greek and five in Latin, is a specific set of case endings. In Greek, the first declension is used almost exclusively for feminine nouns, the second is used mostly for masculine and neuter nouns, while the third is catch-as-catch-can.

Finally, Greek nouns can be singular or plural, and there are different endings for each. A noun in the **singular number** is the name of a single person or thing, unless it is a **collective noun**—the name of a number of persons or things forming one body (*committee, jury, army,* etc.). A noun in the **plural number** is the name of more than one person or thing.

At one time Greek had a special grammatical category called the **dual**. If you wanted to talk about something singular, like Mary or a dog, you used the appropriate singular forms; and if you wanted to talk about three or more, you used the plural. But if it was a question about Mary's eyes or the dog's ears, you used the dual. Apparently the distinction between "one, two, many" proved to be one too many for the Greeks, and the dual was quietly put out to pasture and never heard of again.

Adjectives

Adjectives are easy once you've gotten past the nouns. **Adjectives** are words used to modify nouns or other substantives ("the *good* man," "the *large* crowd," "the *tall* buildings"). Greek adjectives are very much like English ones, except that they often follow the noun they modify. For example, "I am the good shepherd" (John 10:11) is literally "I am the shepherd, the good one." When adjectives are used in this way, they are usually emphatic (as in the English expressions "life *everlasting*" and "God *Almighty*").

Adjectives **agree** with the nouns they modify in gender, number, and case. That is, masculine adjectives go with masculine nouns, plural with plural, singular with singular, nominative with nominative, and so on. Because adjectives use the same endings as nouns, once you have learned the noun declensions you are ready to rumble, at least as far as the *nomen* family is concerned.

Pronouns

As for the other parts of speech, they aren't nearly as difficult as the *nomen* (which, after you get used to it, is not *that* difficult). The *pronomen* class contains words that fill in for their *nomen* cousins. For example, instead of having to say "Sam knew in Sam's heart that Sam should have said to Sam, 'Sam knows, Sam should have worked harder,'" one can say, "Sam knew in *his* heart that *he* should have said to *himself*, 'You know, *you* should have worked harder.'" The members of the *pronomen* class (otherwise known as **pronouns**) also come with the standard issue of cases. Greek comes with a full set of pronouns, including

- the **personal pronoun**: *he*
- the **possessive pronoun**: *my*
- the **reflexive pronoun**: *myself*
- the **reciprocal pronoun**: *one another*
- the **relative pronoun**: *who*
- the **interrogative pronoun**: *who?*
- the **indefinite pronoun**: *someone*
- the **demonstrative pronoun**: *this one*

Verbs

Verbum originally meant "word," as in the apostle John's famous dictum, *In principio erat verbum*, "In the beginning was the Word." Later it came to mean a particular kind of word, the kind that tells you what the action is: a **verb**. Verbs are words that express action, being, or state of being ("I run," "you are," "he is rejoicing"). For the most part, verbs in Greek have the same functions as their English counterparts.

A Greek verb, like a Greek noun, can be viewed as a combination of two basic elements. Again, the stem carries the basic meaning of the word, and the ending or **suffix** handles the details. With the verb, however, you can also add something to the front of the stem (a **prefix**) and something within the stem (an **infix**). This means that the same Greek verb will take on an awful lot of different appearances.

The endings of the verb tell you who the subject is, that is, who is doing or receiving the action expressed by the verb. There are six possibilities, each with a different personal ending:

- **first person** singular: *I*
- **second person** singular: *you*
- **third person** singular: *he, she, it*
- first person plural: *we*
- second person plural: *you*
- third person plural: *they*

Occasionally, English shows traces of the original Indo-European system of stems and endings, as in "I hear," "he hears," to which may be added "thou hearest," which, of course, nobody actually *says* anymore. The endings of a Greek verb also tell you when the action is happening, that is, what **tense** the verb is in, and the kind of action it represents (also known as the **aspect** of the verb). Sometimes Greek manufactures nouns out of verbs by making **infinitives**: "*To hear* your voice again is great." Infinitives are, by definition, "non-finite": they are never limited by person and number as are **finite verbs**, as in "*I hear* your voice."

Verb endings carry two other important pieces of information. The first of these is whether the verb is **active** or **passive**, that is, whether the subject of the verb is doing the action or the action is being done to it. Greek has one verb form for "I hear" (ἀκούω) and another for "I am being heard" (ἀκούομαι). When we use the terms active and passive, we are talking about what grammarians call **voice**. (Greek also contains a **middle voice**, which calls attention to the subject). The second piece of information carried by the verb ending is which **mood** the verb is in—**indicative**, **subjunctive**, **optative**, or **imperative**. Mood takes a bit of explaining, but you can forget about it for the time being. What *is* important to remember now is that verb endings have a lot to tell you, and the wealth of this information is worth every bit of effort you have to expend to acquire it.

Adverbs, Participles, Prepositions, Conjunctions, Interjections

The *adverbium* is the **adverb**, the word that tells you *how* the action is performed—*quickly, slowly, immediately*, and so on. No problem here.

The *participium*, or **participle**, is a cross between a *verbum* and a *nomen*: it has case endings like a noun or adjective, but it has a distinctly verbal flavor. Case endings aside, the Greek participles are not very different from their English counterparts. Consider, for example, the sentence "Going to the beach, I got lost." *Going* is a participle in both English and Greek. The participle is used, however, much more frequently in Greek than in English.

That leaves the *praepositio*, or preposition; the *conjunctio*, or conjunction; and the *interjectio*, or interjection. **Prepositions** are small, suffix-less words that come right before a *nomen* (or *pronomen*) and tell you "where," "how," "when," and sometimes "why," as in "*under* water," "*with* a smile," "*before* the altar," "*for* my retirement," and so on. **Conjunctions** are small, suffix-less words that come between two (or more) of the same parts of speech and join them together, as in "Peter *and* Paul" and "they laughed *but* I cried." **Interjections**, like *ouch*, *hey*, and *oops*, are none of the above. Interjections are usually called **particles** in modern grammar books, "particles" being a catch-all term for the little words that won't squeeze into any other mold.

Organizing the Greek Parts of Speech

When grammarians set out to depict languages, their descriptions are often organized in terms of these eight parts of speech, which, as we have seen, were originally devised to describe Latin. However, not all languages lend themselves to this type of analysis. For example, one analysis of Tamil, a language of south India, lists as many as eleven parts of speech, while another analysis of the same language has only two formal categories: noun and verb.

Of course, some of the differences between grammarians can be reduced to questions of labels. What is called a part of speech by one grammarian may simply be called a subcategory by another, but both will describe its function more or less equivalently. An analysis of languages reveals that verbs and nouns always occur (all languages have them), whereas adjectives and prepositions do not (some languages don't have them), and some languages have their own idiosyncratic parts of speech. Not even all European languages use the identical parts-of-speech system.

All this to say that there's no reason to slavishly follow the Latin grammarians when organizing the Greek parts of speech. In fact, I think it's easiest to divide Greek grammar into two basic systems: a noun (nominal) system, and a verb (verbal) system. Each system has its own subcategories.

- When the noun bears a particular relationship to the rest of the sentence, it is expressed by *case*.
- When you want to make the relationship of the noun to the rest of the sentence more vivid, you use a *preposition*.
- If you want to qualify the noun by some attribute, you use an *adjective*.
- When you want to avoid monotony and repetition, you use a *pronoun*.
- If you desire to represent the thing designated by the noun as particular, you use the *article: the*.[1]

Hence the grammar of the noun includes *cases, prepositions, adjectives, pronouns,* and the *article*.

The verb is the part of speech that makes an assertion.

- When an assertion is subjoined as an auxiliary to another, the *infinitive* or *participle* is used.
- If the assertion is to be varied by certain qualifications, the *adverb* is used.
- In joining one assertion to another, a *conjunction* may be used.
- Finally, the speaker's attitude in the assertion is frequently expressed by a *particle*.

Thus, the verbal system includes *finite verbs, infinitives, participles, adverbs, conjunctions,* and *particles*.

In both of these systems, **morphology**—that part of grammar dealing with the forms of words, their shapes and changes—plays an indispensable role. It is essential that you master these changes before you attempt exegesis, for without such a background exegesis is impossible. The study is enriched and actually becomes a delight when you bear in mind that you are dealing not merely with grammar but with the words of divine revelation. Thus grammar becomes a thrilling means to a divine end. With reasonable study you learn that Greek words are constructed with architectural precision. If your memory of word formation needs to be refreshed, you will save yourself much trouble by reviewing an elementary-level grammar such as my *Learn to Read New Testament Greek,*[2] where you will find sufficient information on these matters.

1. Latin lacks an article, as do modern Russian and Korean. The Greek article was originally a demonstrative pronoun and may be classified as a member of the *pronomen* family. However, because of its importance in New Testament interpretation, it is best treated as a separate part of speech.
2. Expanded ed., Nashville: Broadman & Holman, 1994.

A Word about Words

Because all of the parts of speech are *words*, you will also need to acquire a working vocabulary of Greek if you are going to be able to read the New Testament with facility. How much vocabulary do you need? Obviously, the larger your vocabulary, the more rapidly and extensively you can read. My own suggestion is that you master a *basic vocabulary* of New Testament words. In the Greek New Testament there are about 5,500 vocabulary items, of which 3,600 occur four times or less. This means that you will encounter each of these low-frequency words only once in about 160 pages of the New Testament. On the other hand, 1,100 words occur ten times or more, and these are the words you should attempt to learn by heart.

As for the other 4,400 words, my advice is either guess at their meaning from the context, consult an interlinear, or (preferably) use a good lexicon. Essential tools that will help you acquire a working vocabulary of New Testament Greek are listed in the postscript.

Conclusion

So there you have it—the parts of speech. The inability to recognize them is as much a handicap as not knowing the value of nickels, dimes, quarters, and dollars. This handicap ranges from a fine shade of misunderstanding to outright misinterpretation; its diagnosis and treatment form the staple of this book.

Once again, think of words as bricks, girders, and glass. You put them together to make phrases, clauses, and then sentences. How to construct such edifices is the topic of chapter 2.

For Practice

Put into English the following sentences.

1. οἱ μαθηταὶ ἀκούουσι τοὺς λόγους τῶν προφητῶν.
2. μένομεν μετὰ τῶν ἀδελφῶν ἐν τῇ οἰκίᾳ κατὰ τὸν νόμον.
3. λέγεις λόγους κατὰ τοῦ νόμου τῶν μαθητῶν καὶ τῶν προφητῶν.
4. ἐν τῇ ἐκκλησίᾳ μανθάνομεν τὸν λόγον τοῦ θεοῦ.
5. οἱ νεανίαι τὰ παιδία ἐν τῇ ἐρήμῳ διδάσκουσιν, κύριε.

6. ἔγραφον οἱ ἀπόστολοι τὰς ἐπιστολὰς ἐν τῷ σαββάτῳ.
7. ἐδιδάσκομεν τὸ εὐαγγέλιον τοῖς τέκνοις τῶν στρατιωτῶν.
8. οἱ δὲ ὄχλοι ἤσθιον τοὺς ἄρτους ἐν τῇ ἐρήμῳ καὶ ἔπινον τὸν καρπὸν τῆς ἀμπέλου.
9. ἔσωζεν ὁ Ἰησοῦς αὐτὸς τοὺς ἁμαρτωλοὺς ἐκ τῆς ἁμαρτίας.
10. ὁ ἀπόστολος ἔπεμψε τὸν δοῦλον πρὸς τὴν οἰκίαν σου.
11. οἱ γὰρ μαθηταὶ ἐνήστευον τεσσαράκοντα ἡμέρας.
12. οἱ δοῦλοι αὐτοὶ πέμψουσι ταῦτα τὰ βιβλία εἰς ἐκεῖνο τὸ ἱερόν.
13. ἔπεμψεν ὁ θεὸς ἀγγέλους εἰς τὸ κηρύσσειν αὐτοὺς τοῖς ὄχλοις.
14. μὴ κωλύετε τὰ παιδία βαίνειν πρός με.
15. λέγει αὐτῇ ὁ Ἰησοῦς, Ἀληθές ἐστιν ὅτι οὐκ ἔχεις ἄνδρα. πέντε γὰρ ἄνδρας ἔσχες, καὶ νῦν ὃν ἔχεις οὐκ ἔστίν σου ἀνήρ. λέγει αὐτῷ ἡ γυνή, κύριε, θεωρῶ ὅτι προφήτης εἶ σύ.

Key Terms

accusative case
active voice
adjective
adverb
agreement
aspect
case
collective noun
common gender
conjunction
dative case
declension
demonstrative pronoun
dual
ending
feminine gender
finite verb
first person
gender
genitive case
imperative mood
indefinite pronoun
indicative mood
infinitive
infix

interjection
interrogative pronoun
masculine gender
middle voice
mood
morphology
neuter gender
nominative case
noun
number
optative mood
participle
particle
passive voice
person
personal pronoun
plural
possessive pronoun
prefix
preposition
pronoun
reciprocal pronoun
reflexive pronoun
relative pronoun
second person

singular
stem
subjunctive mood
substantive
suffix

tense
third person
verb
vocative case
voice

2

Group Therapy

The Sentence and Its Parts

N ow that you know the parts of speech, let's talk about how sentences are put together. A **sentence** is a combination of words that express a complete thought: "Life is short." "Is life short?" "How short life is!" How words are joined together to convey meaning is called **syntax**. There can be no sentence, however short, without syntax, however little.

It is by expressing a complete thought that a sentence differs from its subordinate parts, the phrase and the clause. The phrase merely indicates a thought that it does not express completely: "Life *being* short." The clause expresses only part of a thought: "*Because* life is short." Since neither the phrase nor the clause is complete, it leaves the mind in suspension. We ask, "Well, what then?" and wait for some conclusion. But the sentence "Life is short" is complete. All is said and done, and the mind rests. In many respects, therefore, *syntax is the most important part of language study*. Obviously, then, the better we understand how sentences work, the better our thinking about language becomes.

The Sentence: Subject and Predicate

All sentences are composed of two basic parts: the subject and the predicate. The **subject** is the part of the sentence about which an assertion is made by the use of a finite verb: *"Fire* burns." The **predicate** is the part of the sentence that makes an assertion about the subject by using a finite verb: "Fire *burns."*

The finite verb is essential to the sentence. It is the finite verb that completes the sentence, binding it together just as the keystone binds the arch. Neither the participle ("The sky *being* blue") nor the infinitive ("The sky *to be* blue") can complete a sentence. But "The sky *is* blue" (finite verb) is a sentence. There can be no complete assertion without a finite verb.

The **simple subject** of a sentence is a noun or pronoun: *"Christ* died," *"He* died." The **complete subject** is composed of the simple subject and the words that explain or complete its meaning: *"Christ Jesus our Lord and Savior* died."

The **simple predicate** of a sentence is a finite verb or verb phrase: "Christ *died,"* "Christ *has risen."* The **complete predicate** is composed of the simple predicate and the words that explain or complete the meaning: "Christ *died for our sins according to the Scriptures."*

The omission of a word that would be necessary for grammatical completion is called **ellipsis**. If there is no possibility of confusion, the subject may be omitted, as in replies to questions: "Yes," "Maybe." If there is no ambiguity, even the predicate may be omitted: "Blue." This perfectly communicates the idea in the reply to the question "What color is the sky today?"

For complete predication, a finite verb must be used in a simple sentence or in an independent clause. A dependent clause contains a finite verb but is not complete: "If the sky is blue." Despite the finite verb *is,* this statement is incomplete because of the subordinating conjunction *if.* "If the sky is blue," we ask, "what then?" For a complete thought we must have a simple sentence with a finite verb: "The sky is blue." Or the dependent clause with a finite verb must be related to an independent clause that completes the thought: "If the sky is blue, it will not rain today."

Types of Verbs

There are three types of finite verbs. A **transitive verb** transfers an action from the subject of the verb to another person, place, or thing: "Jane *liked* farmer Jones." An **intransitive verb** expresses an action that is limited to the subject of the sentence: "Jane *smiled."* A **linking verb** allows words in the predicate to describe or rename the subject of the sentence: "Jane *was* happy."

The most common linking verbs in the New Testament are εἰμί, γίνο-μαι, and ὑπάρχω. Because of their power to join nouns to other nouns or adjectives, these verbs are called **copulative verbs** (from the Latin verb *copulo*, "I link"). They take the same case after them as before them:

- ὁ . . . ἀγρός [nominative] ἐστιν [linking verb] ὁ κόσμος [nominative], the field is the world (Matt. 13:38)

They are also called **verbs of incomplete predication** because they do not make sense when they stand by themselves (except when used in the sense of *exist*). They must be followed by a noun or an adjective that is called the **complement** because it completes or "fills up" the sense (from the Latin verb *complio*, "I fill up"). This principle is of great importance in reading Greek.

Modifiers

Of course, most statements are not as simple as "The field is the world." Therefore, other elements are generally present in the sentence. Some elements are used to modify the subject, and these are known as **modifiers**. Others, as mentioned, are used to complete the predicate and are called *complements*.

The modifier of the subject may be one or more of the following:

- the definite article: *the* book
- a possessive pronoun: *his* book
- an interrogative pronoun: *which* book?
- an indefinite pronoun: *any* book
- a demonstrative pronoun: *this* book
- an attributive adjective: *large* book
- an adjectival participle: *engaging* book
- an adjectival infinitive: book *to be read*
- a prepositional phrase: book *on the shelf*
- an adjectival clause: book *that makes sense to me*

The complement of the verb may be one or more of the following:

- a direct object: John hit *him*
- a predicate nominative: John is *human*
- a predicate adjective: John is *tall*
- an infinitive: John likes *to sing*
- a cognate accusative: John ran *a race*

- a predicate object: they named John *chairman*
- a predicate genitive: the book was *John's*
- a supplementary participle: John came *running*
- a direct quotation: John said, *"Come!"*
- an indirect quotation: John said that *you should come*
- an indirect object: John gave it *to him*
- an adverb: John ran *quickly*
- a prepositional phrase: John ran *around the track*
- an adverbial clause: John talked *while he was working*
- a genitive absolute: *the storm having stopped,* John went outside
- an adverbial accusative: John waited *hours*

Clearly, words in sentences have rather well-defined duties in their expression of thought.

Classes of Sentences

Sentences themselves may be classified along two different lines: according to their *manner of expressing thought* and their *structure.* As to their manner of expressing thought, sentences may be divided into four classes:

- A **declarative sentence** affirms that something is or is not a fact or a possibility: Christ died for you.
- An **interrogative sentence** asks whether something is or is not a fact: Do you believe this?
- An **imperative sentence** commands or forbids something: Repent and be baptized.
- An **exclamatory sentence** expresses a thought as an exclamation: Praise the Lord!

According to structure, sentences may be divided into four classes:

- A **simple sentence** contains only one subject and one predicate: "Man is mortal," "Elsie smiled today," "John ate the apple as well as the orange." A simple sentence may be long or short. A long sentence may be simple if it contains only one subject and one predicate. Two or more nouns or pronouns may be combined to form one **compound subject**, and two or more verbs may be joined to form one **compound predicate**. But the sentence will still be simple if there is only one compound subject and/or one compound predicate: *"Bill and John* studied together" or "Bill and John *studied and played and laughed* together."

- Two or more simple sentences may be combined to form a **compound sentence**: The days are short, and the nights are long.
- One or more dependent clauses may be joined to a simple sentence to form a **complex sentence**: When I arrived, you were gone.
- One or more dependent clauses may be combined with two or more simple sentences to form a **compound-complex sentence**: The man who wants to buy the car is here, but he is too late.

Phrases

The most important parts of a sentence are the phrase and the clause. A **phrase** is a group of words that cannot stand alone as a sentence because it lacks either a subject or a predicate or both. The words in a phrase work together as a part of speech. For example, they may work together to name a person, place, thing, or idea. In this case the group of words would be called a **noun phrase**. The two most common phrases, however, are the prepositional phrase and the verbal phrase.

Prepositional Phrases

Prepositions are those little words that locate a noun in time, space, or direction. **Prepositional phrases** always begin with a preposition and end with a noun (or another substantive): "around the house," "through the door," "behind him." You have to decide what part of speech these phrases are by looking at how they work in a sentence: "The whole staff went on a vacation." What is the verb? *Went.* What went? *The whole staff.* What does the prepositional phrase tell you? *Where* the staff went. Thus, *on a vacation* is a prepositional phrase that acts as an adverb in this sentence, describing or modifying the verb *went*. Prepositional phrases usually act as adverbs or adjectives. When in doubt, ask yourself what the phrase is telling you in the sentence.

When you are picking apart a sentence in your Greek New Testament, it is usually helpful to put parentheses around prepositional phrases—sometimes they are distracting when you are trying to locate subject and verb. Take, for example, Mark 1:9:

Καὶ ἐγένετο ἐν ἐκείναις ταῖς ἡμέραις ἦλθεν Ἰησοῦς ἀπὸ Ναζαρὲτ τῆς Γαλιλαίας καὶ ἐβαπτίσθη εἰς τὸν Ἰορδάνην ὑπὸ Ἰωάννου.

Now that's a long and somewhat complicated sentence. So gather together the prepositional phrases like this:

Καὶ ἐγένετο (ἐν ἐκείναις ταῖς ἡμέραις) ἦλθεν Ἰησοῦς (ἀπὸ Ναζαρὲτ τῆς Γαλιλαίας) καὶ ἐβαπτίσθη (εἰς τὸν Ἰορδάνην) (ὑπὸ Ἰωάννου).

Now you can clearly identify the verbs *(it was, came, was baptized)* and the subject *(Jesus)*. Then you can translate the basic sentence: "So it was, Jesus came and was baptized." The structure of the sentence is now crystal clear. Finally, mix in the "leftovers": "So it was, in those days Jesus came from Nazareth of Galilee and was baptized in the Jordan by John."

Verbal Phrases

Verbal phrases have verbs in them, but they are not verbs. They act as nouns, adjectives, or adverbs. Both participles and infinitives can form verbal phrases. A participle looks like a verb, but it isn't. You can think of a participle as a verb that acts like an adjective in a sentence. Look at the difference:

- I *had known* that Tom would be famous one day.
- *Known* for his outstanding tenor voice, Tom was famous.

In the first sentence, *had known* is the main verb. *Known* in the second sentence describes Tom; it is adjectival and hence a participle.

If participles are **verbals** (non-finite verbs) that are used as adjectives, infinitives are verbals that are used as nouns, adjectives, or adverbs. Thus:

- A doctor hopes *to help* his patients. [Here *to help* is a noun.]
- Which of these books would be the one *to help* me? [Here *to help* is an adjective modifying the substantive *the one*.]
- My teacher told us jokes *to help* pass the time. [Here *to help* is an adverb that modifies the verb *told*.]

Clauses

Let's now consider clauses. A **clause** is a group of words that forms part of a sentence and that contains a subject and a predicate. There are two types of clauses: independent and dependent. An **independent clause**, also called a **main clause**, makes sense standing alone. A **dependent clause**, also called a **subordinate clause**, is used like an adjective, adverb, or noun. It cannot stand alone because it "depends" on the other clause in the sentence to make sense.

Look at the following sentence: "Jim told me that he was studying Greek." This sentence is made up of two separate clauses: *Jim told me* and *that he was studying Greek.* Both of these clauses have subjects and verbs. But the first clause, *Jim told me,* is the independent or main clause in the sentence because it could stand alone. *That he was studying Greek* is the dependent or subordinate clause: it wouldn't make sense by itself, and the words work together to modify the verb *told.*

A subordinate clause, like a phrase, is used as a part of speech. If it is used as a noun, it is a **noun clause**, or **substantive clause**. If it modifies a substantive it is an **adjectival clause**. If it serves as an adverb it is an **adverbial clause**.

Noun Clauses

A noun clause is a clause that stands in the relationship of a noun to the principal clause or to some other clause in a complex sentence. It may be a subject: *"That he is coming* is certain." It may be an object: "He said *that he was a lawyer.*" It may be a predicate noun: "My hope is *that you will come.*" The infinitive is frequently used in noun clauses in Greek: *"To err* is human" (subject); "We believe him *to be innocent*" (object); "My goal is *to excel*" (complement).

Adjectival Clauses

Adjectival clauses are introduced by the relative pronouns *who, which, that,* and their equivalents *when, where, such as,* and so on. They are called adjectival clauses because they qualify some noun in another clause, just like an adjective. A participle qualifying the noun is also very common.

- This is the one *who sent me*
- This is the person *whom I saw*
- This is the place *where I was born*
- I will do this *when we meet*
- I saw the man *fishing off the pier*

Adverbial Clauses

Adverbial clauses are clauses that stand in the relationship of an adverb to the verb in another clause. Adverbial clauses may be divided into the following classes:

- **final clauses** denote purpose: He ran *that he might get home sooner*
- **temporal clauses** denote time when: He ran *when he got on the road*

- **local clauses** denote place where: He ran *where the road was downhill*
- **causal clauses** denote cause: He ran *because he was late*
- **result clauses** denote consequence: He ran *so that he got home on time*
- **conditional clauses** denote a condition: He ran *if he was late*
- **concessive clauses** denote contrast: He ran *although he was tired*
- **comparative clauses** denote comparison: He ran *as he was accustomed to do*

The names of these clauses are given because they are very common in grammars and commentaries, not because they have any merit in and of themselves.

It is possible to build a sentence with an unlimited number of dependent clauses. Only the inability of the hearer or reader to comprehend the meaning of the sentence limits the complexity with which a person may construct a sentence. For example, Ephesians 1:3–14 is one sentence in Greek. The sentence structure makes perfectly good sense, complex though it may be. In English translations, however, sentences are getting shorter (the NIV uses eight sentences to translate Eph. 1:3–14).

This tendency to shorten sentences raises several important grammatical questions, such as whether clauses exist in a hierarchical relationship. In Ephesians 5:18–21, for instance, there is a break between verse 20 and verse 21 in most English versions, and the Greek participle in verse 21 ("*submitting yourselves* to one another") is translated as an imperative ("*Submit yourselves* to one another"). This seems to miss Paul's point completely. If he had wanted to make a break at verse 21, it would have been the simplest thing in the world to write an imperative. Instead, he writes a durative participle that is just like the participles that precede it, so that we should connect this last participle with the preceding context. Mutual submission (v. 21) is simply the result of being filled with the Holy Spirit (v. 18).

How to Analyze a Sentence

Once you understand how sentences work, sentence analysis becomes fairly straightforward.

1. To begin with, ascertain whether the sentence is a simple sentence with only one essential subject, simple or compound, and one essential predicate, simple or compound. If so, treat the elements of that simple sentence separately. If participial, prepositional, or

other phrases are included in the simple sentence, first treat each phrase as an element of the simple sentence, showing its grammatical relation as a phrase. Then take the words of that phrase separately and show their relation to one another as single words.

2. If the sentence is found to have more than one essential subject and more than one essential predicate, separate the clauses and decide whether they constitute a complex, compound, or compound-complex sentence.

3. Show the relation of the clauses to each other as coordinate and independent in compound and compound-complex sentences, or as independent and dependent in complex sentences.

4. Analyze each clause of the compound, complex, and compound-complex sentences according to the rules and principles established for simple sentences.

Let's return for a moment to Ephesians 5:18–21. The Greek may be analyzed as follows:

καὶ μὴ μεθύσκεσθε οἴνῳ, ἐν ᾧ ἐστιν ἀσωτία,
ἀλλὰ πληροῦσθε ἐν πνεύματι,
λαλοῦντες ἑαυτοῖς [ἐν] ψαλμοῖς καὶ ὕμνοις καὶ ᾠδαῖς πνευματικαῖς,
ᾄδοντες καὶ ψάλλοντες τῇ καρδίᾳ ὑμῶν τῷ κυρίῳ,
εὐχαριστοῦντες πάντοτε ὑπὲρ πάντων ἐν ὀνόματι τοῦ κυρίου ἡμῶν
    Ἰησοῦ Χριστοῦ τῷ θεῷ καὶ πατρί,
ὑποτασσόμενοι ἀλλήλοις ἐν φόβῳ Χριστοῦ.

The main verbs in verse 18 are in the imperative mood: "stop getting drunk" and "keep getting filled." Syntactically, these verbs are marked as being the main ideas. The participles that modify the command to be filled are (1) "speaking," (2) "singing and making melody," (3) "giving thanks," and (4) "submitting yourselves." These participles define what Paul meant by being filled with the Holy Spirit. At this point, a more detailed exegesis of clauses and words takes over.

Conclusion

Let's review what we've covered in this chapter.

• There are two main parts of a sentence: the subject and the predicate. The subject is what the sentence is about. The predicate is everything that is not the subject. It may be a simple verb, or it may be the verb and all the extra things that are talking about the subject.

• A phrase is a group of words that does not have a subject and a verb. The words in a phrase together function as a part of speech.

- A clause is a group of words that includes a subject and a verb.
- A dependent clause cannot stand alone as a sentence.
- An independent clause makes sense by itself.
- A simple sentence has one independent clause—subject and predicate.
- A compound sentence has two or more independent clauses (or simple sentences) joined together with a conjunction.
- A complex sentence has at least one independent clause and at least one dependent clause.
- A compound-complex sentence has one or more dependent clauses combined with two or more simple sentences.

When you use the labels *noun, verb,* and *conjunction,* you are describing or classifying individual words. But when you use a functional vocabulary—*subject, predicate,* and *clause,* for instance—you are describing the words of a sentence in relation to one another. Knowing both vocabularies will help you improve your ability to read the Greek New Testament. You will find them explained, simplified, and perhaps rendered quite interesting in the ensuing pages.

For Practice

Translate the following passage, paying special attention to its clause structure.

Καὶ τοῦτο προσεύχομαι, ἵνα ἡ ἀγάπη ὑμῶν ἔτι μᾶλλον καὶ μᾶλλον περισ-
σεύῃ ἐν ἐπιγνώσει καὶ πάσῃ αἰσθήσει εἰς τὸ δοκιμάζειν ὑμᾶς τὰ διαφέροντα,
ἵνα ἦτε εἰλικρινεῖς καὶ ἀπρόσκοποι εἰς ἡμέραν Χριστοῦ, πεπληρωμένοι
καρπὸν δικαιοσύνης τὸν διὰ Ἰησοῦ Χριστοῦ εἰς δόξαν καὶ ἔπαινον θεοῦ.

Key Terms

adjectival clause
adverbial clause
causal clause
clause
comparative clause
complement
complete predicate
complete subject
complex sentence
compound predicate

compound sentence
compound subject
compound-complex sentence
concessive clause
conditional clause
copulative verb
declarative sentence
dependent clause
ellipsis
exclamatory sentence

final clause
imperative sentence
independent clause
interrogative sentence
intransitive verb
linking verb
local clause
main clause
modifier
noun clause
noun phrase
phrase
predicate
prepositional phrase

result clause
sentence
simple predicate
simple sentence
simple subject
subject
subordinate clause
substantive clause
syntax
temporal clause
transitive verb
verbal phrase
verbals
verbs of incomplete predication

PART 2

The Greeks Had a Word for It

The Greek Noun System

3

Just in Case

Overcoming Declension Apprehension

S ooner or later, generally sooner, the student of Greek discovers that learning a language involves a great deal of memorization. Case endings in nouns are, well, a case in point. "Hey, why should I have to learn so many suffixes?"

Traditional responses to this lament have tended to be in the "if you can't stand the heat, stay out of the kitchen" category. My own advice is: cheer up! The Greek you are studying has actually done away with a number of horrors that you would have had to learn if you were studying Proto-Indo-European, the language from which Greek descended. The Greeks made significant cuts in both the number of cases and the number of **declensions**, that is, the sets of case endings. Besides the nominative, vocative, genitive, dative, and accusative cases, Proto-Indo-European seems to have had *ablative, locative,* and *instrumental* cases as well. The ablative told you where something was from. The locative told you where something was. The instrumental case was used to say *by means of.* The other cases eventually took over these burdens. Moreover, when you consider that the vocative is identical to the nominative in the plural of all nouns, then you really only have four cases to learn (as with modern German). If you take the trouble to learn these forms thoroughly, you are home free, which is more than Greek slaves, women, and children were.

Speaking of Greek culture, the ancient Hellenes thought it useful to talk about cases in geometrical terms. The nominative case was considered to be the vertical radius. The others were considered oblique radii, that is, at an angle. The nominative was therefore known as the "upright" case, and the others as "oblique" cases.

The term *case* itself comes from the Latin verb *cado*, "I fall," by way of the noun *casus*, "a falling." The idea was that when you ran through a complete set of case forms of a noun you started from straight up and down in the nominative, then you fell precipitously through the vocative, genitive, and dative, coming to a crashing halt at the accusative, and not a moment too soon. This process of running—or falling—through the complete set of case forms for a noun was called *declining* (hence the term *declension*). To decline is to turn away from the nominative and make an arc along the path of the genitive, dative, and accusative.

Greek has three declensions, which is another way of saying that there are three possible tracks from nominative to accusative. The first declension, one would think, would be the easiest of all. Actually, the **second declension** is the most straightforward, and, therefore, the one you get to hear about first in most grammar books. It is a general feature of second-declension neuter nouns that they have the same ending for the nominative, vocative, and accusative, making less work for the student of Greek, which is all to the good. With the masculine nouns, the nominative and vocative plurals are all the same. So for all practical purposes, the only time you have to go to the trouble of learning a vocative ending is for masculine singular nouns.

The so-called **first declension** (which is hardly ever studied first) is a little more complicated than the second, but not much. Most of the nouns in the first declension happen to be feminine in gender; the tiny number of exceptions (such as *disciple* and *soldier*) are words that designate male people. All plurals in the first declension, regardless of gender, are declined identically.

The **third declension** is sort of a "leftovers" category. Most books make a big deal out of this declension, with the result that many students are terrified of third-declension nouns. The fact is, if you don't mind having to learn two stems per noun, the third declension is straightforward enough.

If your suffixes are a bit rusty, sample nouns of all three declensions are given in your beginning grammar. Here it is only necessary to note the following features of the declensions.

- The Greek article is declined after the analogy of the first and second declensions.
- Adjectives follow the analogy of nouns. When the masculine and

the feminine differ, they are usually declined in the first and second declensions. When the masculine and the feminine are the same, they are declined in the second and third declensions.

- The great majority of Greek pronouns are found in the first and third declensions. The interrogative, indefinite, and indefinite relative pronouns are declined in the third declension.
- Most participles are found in the first and third declensions. All the middle participles are declined in the first and second declensions.

The Uses of the Greek Cases

You won't get very far in reading the Greek New Testament without a good understanding of how cases work. In fact, about 60 percent of all words in the New Testament use case endings. Moreover, some case uses are notoriously difficult to pin down. This is especially true of the genitive and, to a certain degree, of the dative. The good news is that the other cases are relatively easy to classify.

The significance of the cases of substantives will be treated here under nouns, although adjectives, articles, pronouns, infinitives, and participles also function as substantives. With each of the cases, all you need to know are the major categories.[1]

For each category of cases given below, you will find two clear examples. Remember that the particular shade of a case's usage depends on its relationship to the other words in the sentence. So always look for the classification that seems to fit the author's intention, that is, the one that yields the most natural reading of the verse in context. You must also guard against the danger of overemphasizing subtle points of case. Greek grammar is at best secondary to the context, both literary and historical, in the interpretation of any passage of Scripture. If a proposed meaning cannot be established apart from an appeal to a subtlety of the Greek case system, chances are good that the argument is worthless.

Nominative Case

1. **Subject Nominative**. The nominative is mainly used to name the subject of the sentence. The Greeks, in fact, called it ἡ ὀνομαστικὴ πτῶσις,

---

1. In what follows you will not be tormented with such refinements as "the parenthetical nominative," "the plenary genitive," "the ethical dative," and "the accusative of oaths." These uses of the cases, along with many others, are extremely rare in the New Testament. Though useful in their place, they are relatively unimportant and should not overload the student's memory.

"the naming case." Of course, the subject of the sentence was originally expressed by the verb ending, as in λέγ-ει. But since the meaning of this ending was indefinite (he, she, or it), it was often felt necessary to "name" the subject more definitely, so a noun was used. This noun was simply a further description of the subject that was expressed by the personal ending of the verb.

- ἄλλος ἄγγελος ἦλθεν καὶ ἐστάθη, another *angel* came and stood (Rev. 8:3)
- τὸ φῶς ἐν τῇ σκοτίᾳ φαίνει, *the light* shines in the darkness (John 1:5)

2. **Predicate Nominative**. Linking verbs such as εἰμί, γίνομαι, and ὑπάρχω never take a direct object; they require the nominative case after them. This is called the predicate nominative.

- ὁ λόγος σὰρξ ἐγένετο, the Word became *flesh* (John 1:14)
- ὁ θεὸς ἀγάπη ἐστίν, God is *love* (1 John 4:8)

Note: The predicate nominative is sometimes replaced by εἰς plus the *accusative* in the New Testament. This idiom is frequent in the Greek Old Testament and is probably due to Semitic influence. An example is Mark 10:8: ἔσονται οἱ δύο εἰς σάρκα μίαν, "the two shall become *one flesh*" (literally, *"into one flesh"*).

How can you tell whether the nominative is the subject or the predicate?

1. If only one is a personal, demonstrative, or relative pronoun, it is the subject:

   - οὗτος ἄρχων τῆς συναγωγῆς ὑπῆρχεν, *this man* was a ruler of the synagogue (Luke 8:41)

2. If only one has a definite article, that noun is the subject:

   - θεὸς ἦν ὁ λόγος, *the Word* was God [here θεός is the predicate but is fronted for emphasis: "it was *God* that the Word was"] (John 1:1)

3. If both have the article, translate whichever noun comes first as the subject:

   - ἡ ἁμαρτία ἐστὶν ἡ ἀνομία, *sin* is lawlessness (1 John 3:4)

3. **Nominative of Address**. Whether or not a noun has a separate vocative form, the nominative may be used in direct address, generally with the article.

- ἀπεκρίθη Θωμᾶς καὶ εἶπεν αὐτῷ, Ὁ κύριός μου καὶ ὁ θεός μου, Thomas answered and said to him, "My *Lord* and my *God*" (John 20:28)
- τὰ τέκνα, ὑπακούετε τοῖς γονεῦσιν ὑμῶν, *children,* obey your parents (Eph. 6:1)

4. **Nominative Absolute**. In titles of books, epistolary greetings, doxologies, short exclamations, and proverbial expressions, a nominative may seem as if it has no grammatical connection to the rest of the sentence. This use is also called the **hanging nominative**.

- Παῦλος κλητὸς ἀπόστολος Χριστοῦ Ἰησοῦ, *Paul,* called an apostle of Christ Jesus (1 Cor. 1:1)
- ὁ νικῶν ποιήσω αὐτὸν στῦλον, *the one who overcomes*—I will make him a pillar (Rev. 3:12)

5. **Nominative of Appellation**. The nominative may indicate a proper name in instances where another case seems called for. Inasmuch as the noun is the naming case, this use is quite logical.

- ἐν τῇ Ἑλληνικῇ ὄνομα ἔχει Ἀπολλύων, in Greek he has the name *Apollyon* [here Ἀπολλύων is *nominative* even though it is in apposition to the *accusative* direct object ὄνομα] (Rev. 9:11)
- φωνεῖτέ με ὁ διδάσκαλος καὶ ὁ κύριος, you call me *Teacher* and *Lord* [here διδάσκαλος and κύριος are *nominative* even though they are in apposition to the *accusative* direct object με] (John 13:13)

Vocative Case

The Holy Roman Empire, they say, was neither holy, nor Roman, nor an empire. Likewise, the vocative is not a true case at all, nor is its main function to call someone (the Latin verb *voco* means "I call"). The vocative is simply used for direct address.

Most vocatives are nouns, but some adjectives have vocative forms (e.g., πατὴρ δίκαιε, "Holy Father" [John 17:25]). In the New Testament there is only one instance of a vocative participle (τοῖχε κεκονιαμένε, "you whitewashed wall" [Acts 23:3]). The vocative may be used with the emphatic particle ὦ (as in ὦ ἄνθρωπε, "O man" [Rom. 2:1]), or without ὦ (as in πάτερ, "Father" [John 17:1]). In most printed Greek New Testaments, the vocative is set off by commas:

- τὸ λοιπόν, ἀδελφοί μου, χαίρετε ἐν κυρίῳ, furthermore, *my brothers,* rejoice in the Lord (Phil. 3:1)

- ὦ γύναι, μεγάλη σου ἡ πίστις, O *woman*, great [is] your faith! (Matt. 15:28)

Genitive Case

The genitive case is primarily the describing case. It is older than the adjective and, in fact, is basically adjectival in function. But the genitive is more emphatic than the adjective: "body *of sin*" (Rom. 6:6) carries more semantic weight than "*sinful* body." The genitive is usually related to another substantive, but that relationship is often ambiguous. "The revelation *of Jesus Christ*" (Rev. 1:1) may mean "the revelation *about Jesus Christ*" or "the revelation *from Jesus Christ*." Only the context can tell.

The genitive is a heavy-duty case. It generally has more exegetical significance than the other cases and is subject to a wider variety of interpretations. The result, I regret to say, is often a charley horse between the ears. The more frequent uses of the genitive are listed below.

1. **Genitive of Possession**. The genitive frequently describes a noun from the viewpoint of ownership or possession. A test for the genitive of possession is whether the preposition *of* can be replaced by *belonging to*. As with possessives generally, the term *genitive of possession* should not be identified too closely with ideas of actual ownership or possession.

- Παῦλος ἀπόστολος Χριστοῦ Ἰησοῦ, Paul, an apostle *of Christ Jesus* (2 Cor. 1:1)
- ἴδε ὁ ἀμνὸς τοῦ θεοῦ ὁ αἴρων τὴν ἁμαρτίαν τοῦ κόσμου, Look! The lamb *of God* who takes away the sin *of the world* (John 1:29)

2. **Genitive of Relationship**. This is a special category of the possessive genitive that indicates a family, social, or spiritual relationship. The word defining the relationship is omitted, except for its article, and must be inferred from the context (a masculine article typically stands for *son of*).

- εὗρον Δαυὶδ τὸν τοῦ Ἰεσσαί, I found David *the [son] of Jesse* (Acts 13:22)
- Μαρία ἡ Ἰακώβου, Mary *the [mother] of James* (Luke 24:10)

3. **Partitive Genitive**. A genitive substantive (alone or with ἀπό or ἐκ and always preceded by the definite article) can indicate the whole of which something is a part.

- οἱ λοιποὶ τῶν ἀνθρώπων, the rest *of the men* (Luke 18:11)
- τοὺς πτωχοὺς τῶν ἁγίων, the poor *among the saints* (Rom. 15:26)

4. Subjective Genitive. Linked with an "action noun," the genitive indicates the subject or producer of that action. The action noun is what distinguishes this genitive from the possessive genitive.

- τίς ἡμᾶς χωρίσει ἀπὸ τῆς ἀγάπης τοῦ Χριστοῦ; Who shall separate us from the love *of Christ*? ["love of Christ" implies "Christ loves us"] (Rom. 8:35)
- ἡ ἐπιθυμία τῆς σαρκός, the lust *of the flesh* [i.e., the flesh lusts after something] (1 John 2:16)

5. Objective Genitive. Connected with an "action noun," the genitive indicates the object or recipient of that action.

- ζῆλον θεοῦ ἔχουσιν, they have the zeal *of God* [i.e., "zeal for God"] (Rom. 10:2)
- ἡ δὲ τοῦ πνεύματος βλασφημία οὐκ ἀφεθήσεται, but the blasphemy *of the Spirit* will not be forgiven [i.e., "someone blasphemes the Spirit"] (Matt. 12:31)

Note: Only the *context* (there's that word again!) can tell you whether a genitive that modifies an action noun is subjective or objective. For example, does τὸ κήρυγμα Ἰησοῦ Χριστοῦ (Rom. 16:25) mean "the preaching *that Jesus Christ did*" or "the preaching *about Jesus Christ*"? Or does διὰ πίστεως Ἰησοῦ Χριστοῦ (Rom. 3:22) mean "through faith *in Jesus Christ*" or "through the faith/faithfulness *of Jesus Christ*" (cf. Rom. 3:26; Gal. 2:16, 20)? Such passages continue to befuddle scholars (as well as us lesser mortals).

6. Genitive Absolute. A genitive absolute consists of a clause containing a genitive participle with a substantive that agrees with the participle. However, the genitive absolute clause has only a loose syntactical connection with the rest of the sentence. In English we have a similar construction called the *nominative absolute:* "I being away, my assistant did the work." Here *I* and *being* are respectively pronoun and participle in apposition with each other, but they are grammatically independent of the main clause. In Latin the analogous construction is the *ablative absolute,* of which *Deo volente* ("God willing") is an example. In Greek, the genitive absolute construction is used to indicate some accessory idea. The genitive substantive should be translated as the subject of a dependent clause and the participle as its verb.

- γενομένης ὥρας ἕκτης σκότος ἐγένετο ἐφ᾽ ὅλην τὴν γῆν, *when it was the sixth hour*, darkness came upon the whole land (Mark 15:33)
- καταβαινόντων αὐτῶν ἐκ τοῦ ὄρους ἐνετείλατο αὐτοῖς ὁ Ἰησοῦς, *while they were coming down from the mountain*, Jesus commanded them (Matt. 17:9)

7. **Genitive of Direct Object**. Certain verbs take a direct object in the genitive, including verbs of sensation *(hear, touch, taste, smell)*, emotion, ruling, and accusing.

- οἱ νεκροὶ ἀκούσουσιν τῆς φωνῆς τοῦ υἱοῦ τοῦ θεοῦ, the dead will hear *the voice* of the Son of God (John 5:25)
- τότε ἥψατο τῶν ὀφθαλμῶν αὐτῶν, then he touched their *eyes* (Matt. 9:29)

8. **Genitive of Material or Contents**. The genitive can specify the material out of which something is made or its contents.

- ἐπίβλημα ῥάκους, a patch *of cloth* (Mark 2:21)
- ποτήριον ὕδατος, a cup *of water* (Mark 9:41)

9. **Descriptive Genitive**. A quality that could have been described by an adjective might be put in the genitive. This use of the genitive is nearest to the basic meaning of the case.

- καρδία πονηρὰ ἀπιστίας, an evil heart *of unbelief* [i.e., "an evil, unbelieving heart"] (Heb. 3:12)
- λόγοις τῆς χάριτος, with words *of grace* [i.e., "with graceful words"] (Luke 4:22)

10. **Genitive of Apposition**. A genitive may follow a substantive of any case and further identify that substantive. This use is also called the **epexegetical genitive**. To tell whether the genitive in question is a genitive of apposition, see if you can replace *of* with *which is, that is,* or *namely*.

- ὁ δοὺς ἡμῖν τὸν ἀρραβῶνα τοῦ πνεύματος, the one who gave us the down payment *of the Spirit* [= *which is the Spirit*] (2 Cor. 5:5)
- ἔλεγεν περὶ τοῦ ναοῦ σώματος αὐτοῦ, he was speaking about the temple *of his body* [= *which is his body*] (John 2:21)

Note: A much debated text is Ephesians 4:9: καὶ κατέβη εἰς τὰ κατώτερα μέρη τῆς γῆς. Does this mean "he [Christ] also descended into the lower parts of the earth [that is, to the underworld]," or "he also descended into the lower parts, that is, the earth"? The latter translation would be a reference either to Christ's incarnation or (more probably) to the descent of the Holy Spirit at Pentecost. Other significant passages possibly involving a genitive of apposition include Matthew 12:39 ("the sign *of Jonah*"), Acts 2:38 ("the gift *of the Holy Spirit*"), 2 Corinthians 1:22 ("the pledge *of the Spirit*"), Revelation 2:10 ("the crown *of life*"), and Ephesians 2:15 ("the law *of the commandments*").

11. **Genitive of Comparison**. The substantive with which a comparison is made is often in the genitive (comparison is also made with ἤ).

- ἰσχυρότερός μού ἐστιν, he is stronger *than I* (Matt. 3:11)
- πολλῶν στρουθίων διαφέρετε, you are more valuable *than many sparrows* (Luke 12:7)

12. **Genitive of Time**. A genitive may indicate the time within which an event occurs. Time in Greek may also be expressed by the dative (point of time) and the accusative (extent or duration of time).

- οὗτος ἦλθεν πρὸς αὐτὸν νυκτός, he came to him *during the night* (John 3:2)
- νηστεύω δὶς τοῦ σαββάτου, I fast twice *during the week* (Luke 18:12)

13. **Genitive of Measure**. This use of the genitive indicates how much or how far.

- ἠγοράσθητε γὰρ τιμῆς, for you were bought *for a price* (1 Cor. 6:20)
- οὐχὶ δηναρίου συνεφώνησάς μοι; didn't you agree with me *for a denarius*? (Matt. 20:13)

14. **Genitive of Source**. Source may be indicated by the genitive alone or with ἀπό or ἐκ.

- διὰ τῆς παρακλήσεως τῶν γραφῶν, through the comfort *from the Scriptures* (Rom. 15:4)
- ἵνα ἡ ὑπερβολὴ τῆς δυνάμεως ᾖ τοῦ θεοῦ καὶ μὴ ἐξ ἡμῶν, in order that the surpassing power might be *from God* and not *from us* (2 Cor. 4:7)

Dative Case

The root idea of the dative case is that of personal interest, pointing out the person *to* or *for* whom something is done. The dative has several important uses.

1. **Dative of Indirect Object**. This is the most common use of the dative. It names the person or thing to which something is done or given.

- πάντα ἀποδώσω σοι, I will repay *you* all things (Matt. 18:26)
- προσέφερον αὐτῷ παιδία, they were bringing children *to him* (Mark 10:13)

2. **Instrumental Dative**. The dative (with or without ἐν) can show the instrument or means by which something is accomplished. The English prepositions *with, by,* or *by means of* may be used to translate this use of the dative.

- κατακόπτων ἑαυτὸν λίθοις, slashing himself *with stones* (Mark 5:5)
- τῇ γὰρ χάριτί ἐστε σεσῳσμένοι, for *by [that] grace* you are saved (Eph. 2:8)

3. **Locative Dative**. The locative dative (with or without ἐν) indicates the place or sphere in which something happens. Prepositions such as *in, on, at, upon,* and *beside* are often used to translate the locative dative into English.

- εἴασεν πάντα τὰ ἔθνη πορεύεσθαι ταῖς ὁδοῖς αὐτῶν, he permitted all the nations to walk *in their ways* (Acts 14:16)
- ἐπέθηκαν αὐτοῦ τῇ κεφαλῇ, they put it *on his head* (John 19:2)

4. **Dative of Time**. This is a special use of the locative dative. The word in the dative indicates a particular point of time within a succession of events.

- τῇ τρίτῃ ἡμέρᾳ ἐγερθήσεται, *on the third day* he will be raised (Matt. 20:19)
- τῇ . . . μίᾳ τῶν σαββάτων, *on the first [day]* of the week (Luke 24:1)

5. **Dative of Possession**. Possession is occasionally shown by the dative along with the linking verbs εἰμί, γίνομαι, or ὑπάρχω.

- καὶ οὐκ ἦν αὐτοῖς τέκνον, and *they* had no child [literally, "there was not a child *to them*"] (Luke 1:7)
- μονογενής μοί ἐστιν, he is *my* only son [literally, "he is an only son *to me*"] (Luke 9:38)

6. **Dative of Direct Object**. Some verbs that emphasize a close personal relationship take a direct object in the dative case.

- ὑπακούουσιν αὐτῷ, they obey *him* (Mark 1:27)
- δουλεύω νόμῳ θεοῦ, I serve God's *law* (Rom. 7:25)

7. **Dative of Reference**. This use of the dative shows an interest that is more remote than the indirect object.

- τῇ ἁμαρτίᾳ ἀπέθανεν, He died *to sin* (Rom. 6:10)
- ἵνα τῷ σταυρῷ τοῦ Χριστοῦ μὴ διώκωνται, so that they might not be persecuted *for the cross* of Christ (Gal. 6:12)

8. **Dative of Advantage or Disadvantage**. In these uses of the dative the idea of personal interest is emphasized. The English preposition *for* is ordinarily used in translating the dative of advantage, while the preposition *against* is used for the dative of disadvantage.

- ἡτοιμασμένην ὡς νύμφην κεκοσμημένην τῷ ἀνδρὶ αὐτῆς, prepared as a bride adorned *for her husband* (Rev. 21:2)
- ἡ . . . Ἡρῳδιὰς ἐνεῖχεν αὐτῷ, Herodias had a grudge *against him* (Mark 6:19)

9. **Dative of Manner**. The dative case may show the manner in which the action of the verb is carried out.

- πᾶσα δὲ γυνὴ προσευχομένη . . . ἀκατακαλύπτῳ τῇ κεφαλῇ, but every woman praying *with an uncovered head* (1 Cor. 11:5)
- εἰ ἐγὼ χάριτι μετέχω, if I partake *with gratitude* (1 Cor. 10:30)

10. **Dative of Association**. Many times the dative will appear alone in a construction that could have σύν plus the dative.

- εἰς ἀπάντησιν ἡμῖν, unto a meeting *with us* (Acts 28:15)
- ὡμίλει αὐτῷ, he spoke *with him* (Acts 24:26)

11. **Dative of Agency**. As the personal agent of a passive verb, the dative of agency is similar to ὑπό plus the genitive.

- οὐδὲν ἄξιον θανάτου ἐστὶν πεπραγμένον αὐτῷ, nothing worthy of death has been done *by him* (Luke 23:15)
- ὤφθη ἀγγέλοις, he was seen *by angels* (1 Tim. 3:16)

Accusative Case

Of the oblique cases, the accusative is by far the one most frequently used in the New Testament. The basic idea of the accusative is that of extension or limitation. It describes the extent or limitation to which a quality or an act or movement is conceived as applying.

1. **Accusative of Direct Object**. In its most common usage, the accusative receives the action of a transitive verb. There is generally a distinct reason for using some other case instead (see the *genitive of direct object* and the *dative of direct object*). Greek usage is very much like English as regards the direct object of a transitive verb, although many verbs that are treated as transitive in English are intransitive in Greek and vice versa. For these points the lexicon must be consulted.

- ἐδίδασκεν τοὺς ὄχλους, he was teaching *the crowds* (Luke 5:3)
- καὶ ἐφοβήθησαν φόβον μέγαν, and they feared *a great fear* [or "feared exceedingly"; here the direct object is a cognate of the verb and is often called a *cognate accusative*] (Mark 4:41)

2. **Double Accusative**. Certain verbs (e.g., *make, teach, remind, consider, receive, ask, reckon, prove, call, name, appoint*) take two accusatives.

- ἤρξατο διδάσκειν αὐτοὺς πολλά, he began to teach *them many things* (Mark 6:34)
- εἶχον Ἰωάννην ὑπερέτην, they had *John [as] an assistant* (Acts 13:5)

3. **Accusative of Time**. Extent of time is indicated by the accusative.

- εἶδον τὰ ἔργα μου τεσσεράκοντα ἔτη, they saw my works *for forty years* (Heb. 3:9–10)
- τί ὧδε ἐστήκατε ὅλην τὴν ἡμέραν ἀργοί; why are you standing here idle *all day?* (Matt. 20:6)

Note: A "time" noun *(hour, day, year)* may indicate something distinctive about the time of an action, depending on its case:

Genitive	*kind* of time	(he taught *by day*)
Dative	*point* of time	(he taught *on the third day*)
Accusative	*extent* of time	(he taught *for twelve days*)

These categories are not airtight: both the nominative (Luke 9:28) and the dative (Luke 1:75) can denote extent of time.

4. **Adverbial Accusative**. The word in the accusative answers the question, "To what does the verb relate?" A special use of the adverbial accusative is to express the subject of an infinitive.

- πᾶς ὁ ἀγωνιζόμενος πάντα ἐγκρατεύεται, everyone who struggles exercises self-control *in all things* (1 Cor. 9:25)
- μετὰ τὸ παθεῖν αὐτὸν, after *he* suffered (Acts 1:3)

Conclusion

My (modest) objective in this chapter has been to introduce you to the most important Greek case ideas. Don't let them bewilder you. They are dear friends and close relatives of our own familiar English. Like the pots and pans in a friend's kitchen, the way they are arranged, their sizes, and their uses may differ from your own, but they are still tools you can learn to use. Whichever one (or ones) you start with, look it squarely in the eye, seize it firmly by the hand, and start using it at once in reading your Greek New Testament. Soon you'll find that the cases in Greek are like new friends who take you into their homes, show you around, and treat you as though you were one of the family.

For Practice

Put into English the following passage.

Παῦλος καὶ Σιλουανὸς καὶ Τιμόθεος τῇ ἐκκλησίᾳ Θεσσαλονικέων ἐν θεῷ πατρὶ καὶ κυρίῳ Ἰησοῦ Χριστῷ, χάρις ὑμῖν καὶ εἰρήνη. Εὐχαριστοῦμεν τῷ θεῷ πάντοτε περὶ πάντων ὑμῶν μνείαν ποιούμενοι ἐπὶ τῶν προσευχῶν ἡμῶν, ἀδιαλείπτως μνημονεύοντες ὑμῶν τοῦ ἔργου τῆς πίστεως καὶ τοῦ κόπου τῆς ἀγάπης καὶ τῆς ὑπομονῆς τῆς ἐλπίδος τοῦ κυρίου ἡμῶν Ἰησοῦ Χριστοῦ ἔμπροσθεν τοῦ θεοῦ καὶ πατρὸς ἡμῶν, εἰδότες, ἀδελφοὶ ἠγαπημένοι ὑπὸ τοῦ θεοῦ, τὴν ἐκλογὴν ὑμῶν, ὅτι τὸ εὐαγγέλιον ἡμῶν οὐκ ἐγενήθη εἰς ὑμᾶς ἐν λόγῳ μόνον ἀλλὰ καὶ ἐν δυνάμει καὶ ἐν πνεύματι ἁγίῳ καὶ ἐν πληροφορίᾳ πολλῇ, καθὼς οἴδατε οἷοι ἐγενήθημεν ἐν ὑμῖν δι᾿ ὑμᾶς.

Key Terms

accusative
accusative of direct object
accusative of time
adverbial accusative
dative
dative of advantage
    or disadvantage
dative of agency
dative of association
dative of direct object
dative of indirect object
dative of manner
dative of possession
dative of reference
dative of time
declension
descriptive genitive
double accusative
epexegetical genitive
first declension
genitive
genitive absolute
genitive of apposition

genitive of comparison
genitive of direct object
genitive of material or contents
genitive of measure
genitive of possession
genitive of relationship
genitive of source
genitive of time
hanging nominative
instrumental dative
locative dative
nominative
nominative absolute
nominative of address
nominative of appellation
objective genitive
partitive genitive
predicate nominative
second declension
subject nominative
subjective genitive
third declension

For Further Reading

Robertson 446–543
Dana and Mantey 65–95
BDF 79–109
Zerwick 9–26
Wallace 31–205

4

The Good, the Bad, and the Ugly

Adjectives Large and Small

It would be a mighty dreary world without adjectives. In fact, it would be just a world, because there'd be no words like *dreary*. You may have thought that nouns were fascinating, but adjectives—well, that's another story. In grammar and writing, the fun really starts when you get to *describe* things, and that's where adjectives come in. The New Testament writers knew this well.

> δεῖ οὖν τὸν ἐπίσκοπον ἀνεπίλημπτον εἶναι, μιᾶς γυναικὸς ἄνδρα, νηφάλιον σώφρονα κόσμιον φιλόξενον διδακτικόν, μὴ πάροινον μὴ πλήκτην, ἀλλὰ ἐπιεικῆ ἄμαχον ἀφιλάργυρον.

> Now an overseer must be *above reproach,* the husband of *one* wife, *sober, sensible, respectable, hospitable, able to teach,* not *given to drink* or a violent person, but *gentle, not quarrelsome,* and *not a lover of money.* (1 Tim. 3:2–3)

Here Paul uses *eleven* adjectives in just two short verses.

Perhaps to avoid stacking up adjectives in this way, most modern editors and language instructors advise the use of as few adjectives as possible. According to one manual of instruction, "the work of skilled writers shows that verbs and nouns contribute more than adjectives in giving a reader a vivid and real impression." Yet in this very statement the key words are *skilled, vivid,* and *real*—all adjectives. Take almost any liter-

57

ary passage, be it in the New Testament or a modern work, and rewrite it, omitting the modifiers, and see what you have left. Try, for instance, taking the adjectives out of this stanza from Coleridge's famous "Rime of the Ancient Mariner":

> The fair breeze blew, the white foam flew,
> The furrow followed free;
> We were the first that ever burst
> Into that silent sea.

If this were reduced to "The breeze blew, the foam flew, the furrow followed; we were the first that ever burst into the sea," the spell is gone. It's true—the **adjective** is as important a part of speech as its governing noun: it defines or gives sharpness to what would otherwise be a general, vague term.

The Function of Adjectives

How, then, do adjectives work?

- Most English adjectives can go before nouns and modify them: "*big* houses," "a *fast* car," "an *original* idea." Adjectives that can go in this position are called *attributive adjectives.*
- Sometimes adjectives follow linking verbs, of which the main example is the verb *be.* Adjectives that can go in this position are called *predicate adjectives:* "The houses were *big*," "Jim's car was *fast*," "That idea is *original.*"
- Then there are *substantival adjectives*—adjectives that function like nouns, as in the title to this chapter (taken from the Clint Eastwood movie): "The Good, the Bad, and the Ugly."

Some English adjectives, such as *mere* and *latter,* can only be attributive: "the *latter* example" is acceptable, but "the example was *latter*" is not. Other English adjectives are used mainly in the predicate position. These include *asleep, awake, alive,* and *afloat.* Thus, "the baby's *asleep*" is grammatical, but "an *asleep* baby" is not (instead we say "a *sleeping* baby"). Most English adjectives, however, are both attributive and predicate, that is, they can go in either one of the typical adjectival positions.

In older English it was common to put attributive adjectives after nouns, especially in poetry: "He arrived at the palace *grand.*" In modern English this is possible only in a few fixed phrases: "secretary *general*," "poet *laureate*," "president *elect*," "joy *unspeakable*," "court *martial*" (i.e., a *military* court), "notary *public*" (i.e., a *public* notary). Greek adjectives enjoy the same flexibility of being pre- or postpositioned.

Most languages have adjectives, though some have very few. A few languages have no adjectives at all, such as Acehnese, a language spoken in northern Sumatra. Greek is an adjective-loving language, though the adjective is not the only device in Greek whose purpose is to describe. As we saw in chapter 3, the same force belongs to the genitive, especially the *genitive of description* and the *genitive of apposition*.

The Greek adjective began its career as a noun. This usage survives in English: "this is an *apple*" (noun), but "this is an *apple* cart" (adjective). Gradually a distinct class of words became "adjectives." Their Greek name, ὀνόματα ἐπίθετα, aptly calls attention to their function as descriptive words or "epithets" that are added to nouns much as a label is added to a bottle to describe its contents.

Unlike the admirable simplicity of the uninflected English adjective, Greek adjectives are declined on the analogy of the noun and are required to agree with their nouns in gender, number, and case.

- The majority of Greek adjectives have three endings, that is, one for each gender: ἀγαθός, ἀγαθή, ἀγαθόν. Note that the masculine and neuter belong to the second declension, while the feminine—the middle form—belongs to the first.
- Another class of adjectives of three endings belongs to the first and third declensions: πᾶς, πᾶσα, πᾶν.
- A group of adjectives belonging to the second declension has only two endings: ἄπιστος, ἄπιστον.
- Yet another group belonging to the third declension has two endings: ἀληθής, ἀληθές.

You can update your data bank of adjective declensions by consulting your first-year grammar.

Uses of the Greek Adjective

The Greek adjective is very much like its English cousin. It has four distinct uses: attributive, predicate, substantival, and adverbial.

1. The **attributive adjective** modifies a substantive by "attributing" a quality to it. The attributive adjective can usually be recognized by the article that precedes it: τὸ ζῶν ὕδωρ, "the *living* water." Frequently the adjective follows the noun: τὸ ὕδωρ τὸ ζῶν, "the *living* water" [literally, "the water, the *living*"] (John 4:11). The meaning is the same, but the

latter position is emphatic. Occasionally the attributive adjective is used without an article, as in ὕδωρ ζῶν, *"living* water" (John 4:10). In such constructions the noun also does not have the article. Further examples of the attributive adjective include:

- ἀπὸ τῆς πρώτης ἡμέρας ἄχρι τοῦ νῦν, from the *first* day until now (Phil. 1:5)
- ἐγώ εἰμι ὁ ποιμὴν ὁ καλός, I am the *good* shepherd (John 10:11)
- οὗτός ἐστιν ὁ ἀληθινὸς θεός, this is the *true* God (1 John 5:20)
- ὡς ἔχρισεν αὐτὸν ὁ θεὸς πνεύματι ἁγίῳ, how God anointed him with the *Holy* Spirit (Acts 10:38)
- μόνῳ σοφῷ θεῷ, to the *only wise* God (Rom. 16:27)
- δώσουσιν σημεῖα μεγάλα καὶ τέρατα, they will provide *great* signs and wonders (Matt. 24:24)

2. The **predicate adjective** makes a statement (or "predicates" something) about the subject: τὸ φρέαρ ἐστὶν βαθύ, "the well is *deep*" (John 4:11). A linking verb may or may not accompany the adjective: μακάριοι οἱ πτωχοὶ τῷ πνεύματι, *"Blessed* [are] the poor in spirit" (Matt. 5:3). The predicate adjective occurs with all tenses and moods, as well as with the infinitive and participle. Note that the predicate adjective is *never* immediately preceded by an article:

- οὐκ εἰμὶ ἱκανὸς καλεῖσθαι ἀπόστολος, I am not *worthy* to be called an apostle (1 Cor. 15:9)
- ἔσται πάντων ἔσχατος, he will be *last* of all (Mark 9:35)
- ἄξιος ὁ ἐργάτης τοῦ μισθοῦ αὐτοῦ, a worker [is] *worthy* of his wages (1 Tim. 5:18)
- ἵνα ἦτε τέλειοι καὶ ὁλόκληροι, in order that you may be *perfect* and *complete* (James 1:4)
- δι᾽ ἧς ἐμαρτυρήθη εἶναι δίκαιος, by which it was testified that he was *righteous* (Heb. 11:4)
- δι᾽ ὑμᾶς ἐπτώχευσεν πλούσιος ὤν, he became poor for us, even though he was *rich* (2 Cor. 8:9)
- καὶ εὐχάριστοι γίνεσθε, and be *grateful* (Col. 3:15)
- τί μέ λέγεις ἀγαθόν; why do you call me *good?* (Luke 18:19)

3. The adjective may recover its original substantival character and perform the function of a noun. This is called the **substantival adjective**. The adjective is immediately preceded by the article if one is present.

- ῥῦσαι ἡμᾶς ἀπὸ τοῦ πονηροῦ, deliver us from *the evil one* (Matt. 6:13)

- ὁ δίκαιος ἐκ πίστεως ζήσεται, *the just* will live by faith (Gal. 3:11)
- ὑμεῖς χρῖσμα ἔχετε ἀπὸ τοῦ ἁγίου, you have an anointing from *the Holy One* (1 John 2:20)
- ἀγαπητέ, μὴ μιμοῦ τὸ κακὸν ἀλλὰ τὸ ἀγαθόν, *beloved*, do not imitate *evil* but *good* (3 John 11)
- ἀπὸ μικροῦ ἕως μεγάλου αὐτῶν, from *the least* to *the greatest* of them (Heb. 8:11)

4. Sometimes the adjective modifies a verbal idea rather than a substantive and therefore functions like an adverb. This is known as the **adverbial adjective**. The adjective will usually be in the accusative case, though the nominative, genitive, and dative cases are also found.

- εὑρέθη Ἰησοῦς μόνος, Jesus was found *alone* (Luke 9:36)
- τοῦ λοιποῦ κόπους μοι μηδεὶς παρεχέτω, *from now on*, let no one cause me trouble (Gal. 6:17)
- καθὼς προέγραψα ἐν ὀλίγῳ, just as I wrote before *briefly* (Eph. 3:3)
- ἔτι μικρὸν μεθ' ὑμῶν εἰμι, yet *a little while* I am with you (John 13:33)

The Comparison of Adjectives

Comparison is the method by which an adjective expresses a greater or lesser degree of the same quality. Most adjectives are capable of expressing three degrees of the quality indicated, known as **positive degree** ("large"), **comparative degree** ("larger"), and **superlative degree** ("largest"). The positive degree expresses simply the quality of an object without reference to another object: "your horse is *large*." The comparative degree shows that an object has more or less of a quality than some other object or objects with which it is compared: "your horse is *larger* than mine." The superlative degree expresses the greatest or least amount or intensity of a quality that is found among all the objects compared: "your horse is *the largest* in the stable."

The comparative and superlative degrees are expressed in Greek by adding -τερος and -τατος to the stem of adjectives of the second declension and to the stem of those adjectives ending in ης in the third declension. Sometimes the final o of the stem is lengthened to ω. For example:

	Positive	**Comparative**	**Superlative**
righteous	δίκαιος	δικαιότερος	δικαιότατος
strong	ἰσχυρός	ἰσχυρότερος	ἰσχυρότατος
wise	σοφός	σοφώτερος	σοφώτατος

Some adjectives form their degrees of comparison irregularly:

	Positive	Comparative	Superlative
good	ἀγαθός	κρείσσων	κράτιστος
great	μέγας	μείζων	μέγιστος

An adjective in the comparative degree is followed either by a noun or pronoun in the genitive case, or by ἤ ("than") followed by a noun or pronoun in the same case as the noun or pronoun with which the adjective agrees: σοφώτερός ἐστιν τοῦ υἱοῦ or σοφώτερός ἐστιν ἢ ὁ υἱός, "he is wiser than his son."

Strictly speaking, the comparative degree indicates a contrast between two elements, while the superlative degree indicates a contrast among three or more elements: "Who was stronger, King Kong or Godzilla?" "Who is the stupidest of the Three Stooges?" In the Greek of the New Testament, however, there is a tendency to "push the degrees down." The positive adjective tends to be used for the comparative, and the comparative for the superlative. Thus, superlative adjectives rarely have the true superlative idea. Instead, the idea is usually **elative**, with the meaning *very:* ὄχλος πλεῖστος (Mark 4:1) means "a *very large* crowd," not "the *largest* crowd." An exception to this rule is ὕψιστος, "highest." The elative sense would be "very high," but God is always regarded as "the Highest" (see Matt. 21:9; Mark 5:7). The tendency to use the comparative for the superlative is seen in 1 Corinthians 13:13. Here the comparative form is used with three objects: "now abide faith, hope, love; but the *greater* of these is love." The meaning, however, is clear: "the *greatest* of these is love."

Knowing how comparison works with Greek adjectives can be very useful in translation and interpretation. Look for the following uses:

Positive Adjectives

- ἀποστυγοῦντες τὸ πονηρόν, κολλώμενοι τῷ ἀγαθῷ, hating *the evil*, clinging to *the good* (Rom. 12:9)
- ὁ νόμος πνευματικός ἐστιν, the Law is *spiritual* (Rom. 7:14)
- ἡ ἐντολὴ ἁγία καὶ δικαία καὶ ἀγαθή, the commandment [is] *holy* and *righteous* and *good* (Rom. 7:12)
- καλόν σοί ἐστιν μονόφθαλμον εἰς τὴν ζωὴν εἰσελθεῖν, it is *better* for you to enter life with one eye [here the positive adjective καλόν is used as a comparative] (Matt. 18:9)
- αὕτη ἐστὶν ἡ μεγάλη καὶ πρώτη ἐντολή, this is *the greatest* and *most important* commandment [here the positive adjectives μεγάλη and πρώτη are used as superlatives] (Matt. 22:38)

Comparative Adjectives

- τὸ μωρὸν τοῦ θεοῦ σοφώτερον τῶν ἀνθρώπων ἐστιν, the foolishness of God is *wiser* than people (1 Cor. 1:25)
- μείζων ὁ προφητεύων ἢ ὁ λαλῶν γλώσσαις, *greater* is the one who prophesies than the one who speaks in tongues (1 Cor. 14:5)
- μείζονα ταύτης ἀγάπην οὐδεὶς ἔχει, no one has *greater* love than this (John 15:13)
- Ἰησοῦς πλείονας μαθητὰς ποιεῖ καὶ βαπτίζει ἢ Ἰωάννης, Jesus is making and baptizing *more* disciples than John (John 4:1)
- ζηλοῦτε δὲ τὰ χαρίσματα τὰ μείζονα, but you are seeking the *most spectacular* gifts [here the comparative adjective μείζονα is used as a superlative] (1 Cor. 12:31)

Superlative Adjectives

- Ἰησοῦ υἱὲ τοῦ θεοῦ τοῦ ὑψίστου, Jesus, Son of the *Highest* God (Luke 8:28)
- ἐγὼ γάρ εἰμι ὁ ἐλάχιστος τῶν ἀποστόλων, for I am the *least* of the apostles (1 Cor. 15:9)
- μετάγεται ὑπὸ ἐλαχίστου πηδαλίου, [ships] are turned by a *very small* rudder [here the superlative adjective ἐλαχίστου is used in an elative sense] (James 3:4)

Numerals as Adjectives

Numerals are a special class of adjectives. They may be divided into two main classes: cardinals and ordinals. A **cardinal** is any number used in counting (*one, two, three,* etc.). An **ordinal** indicates order or succession (*first, second, third,* etc.). Numerals do not permit comparison.

- οἱ γὰρ πάντες ἐκ τοῦ ἑνὸς ἄρτου μετέχομεν, for we all partake of the *one* loaf (1 Cor. 10:17)
- ἐποίησεν δώδεκα, he appointed *twelve* (Mark 3:14)
- ἀναιρεῖ τὸ πρῶτον ἵνα τὸ δεύτερον στήσῃ, he takes away the *first* in order that he may establish the *second* (Heb. 10:9)
- οὗτος ὁ θάνατος ὁ δεύτερός ἐστιν, this is the *second* death (Rev. 20:14)

Adjectives at Play

Greek adjectives, like English ones, are a playground of excitement. Step right through the gate and watch some of the strangest words as they clamber over the jungle gyms and careen down the sliding boards: *aqueous, abstemious, adventitious, detartrated, parecious, quadriliteral.*

If you're sitting there scratching *your* head, imagine what the Ephesians must have thought when they encountered Paul's ἐλαχιστότερος (Eph. 3:8). They knew that ἐλάχιστος meant "least," but Paul, wanting to express his sense of personal unworthiness, added a *comparative* ending to this *superlative* stem. As ἐλάχιστος is already a superlative, Paul's word can only mean "leaster"! Or take John's *double* comparative μειζοτέραν, "more greater" (3 John 4). Perhaps this is best rendered, as in Pidgin English, "mo' betta." Or how about that strange and wonderful expression ἅγια ἁγίων, "Holy of Holies" (Heb. 9:3). Here the *positive* adjective is most likely being used for the *superlative*: "Holiest Place." If that's the case, shouldn't we translate βασιλεὺς βασιλέων and κύριος κυρίων "Kingliest King" and "Lordliest Lord"? Watch out for those merry-go-rounds and seesaws!

Conclusion

If you have read this *brief* chapter carefully, you are a *diligent* and *responsible* student (and, possibly, *tall, dark,* and *handsome* to boot). At *least* you are *able* to understand how those *fascinating* words called adjectives work—and play.

For Practice

Put into English the following sentences.

1. οὐκ ἔστιν δοῦλος μείζων τοῦ κυρίου αὐτοῦ.
2. αὕτη νεωτέρα ἐστιν ἢ αὐτῆς ἡ ἀδελφή.
3. τὸ ἀσθενὲς τοῦ θεοῦ ἰσχυρότερον τῶν ἀνθρώπων.
4. οἱ υἱοὶ τοῦ αἰῶνος τούτου φρονιμώτεροι τῶν υἱῶν τοῦ φωτός.
5. ὁ πατήρ μου πάντων μεῖζόν ἐστιν.
6. δώδεκα μῆνές ἐν ἔτει εἰσιν.
7. ἐγώ εἰμι ἡ ἄμπελος ἡ ἀληθινή, καὶ ὁ πατήρ μου ὁ γεωργός ἐστιν.
8. οὗτοι οἱ λόγοι πιστοὶ καὶ ἀληθινοί.
9. μεγάλη σου ἡ πίστις.
10. οἱ δώδεκα σὺν Ἰησοῦ ἦσαν ἐν πόλει τινί.
11. δύο υἱοὶ ἀνθρώπῳ τινι ἦσαν.
12. τὸ σῶμα χωρὶς πνεύματος νεκρόν ἐστιν.
13. μεγάλη ἡ ἀγάπη τοῦ θεοῦ.
14. πιστὸς ὁ λόγος.

15. οὗτος μέγας κληθήσεται ἐν τῇ βασιλείᾳ τῶν οὐρανῶν.
16. πολλὰ τὰ σκεύη τοῦ ἱεροῦ.
17. ἡ πίστις χωρὶς ἔργων νεκρά ἐστιν.
18. πολλοὶ τυφλοὶ ἐν τῇ ὁδῷ εἰσιν.
19. διὰ τοῦτο οἱ υἱοὶ τοῦ θεοῦ μακαριώτεροι.

Key Terms

adjectives
adverbial adjective
attributive adjective
cardinal
comparative degree
comparison of adjectives
elative

numerals
ordinal
positive degree
predicate adjective
substantival adjective
superlative degree

For Further Reading

Robertson 650–75
Dana and Mantey 115–22
BDF 125–29
Zerwick 47–51
Wallace 291–314

5

Woe Is I

Overcoming Pronoun Paranoia

Pronouns are those remarkably handy little words (*I, you, she, it, them,* etc.) that spare us the trouble of having to repeat the actual name of a person, place, or thing each time we refer to a person, place, or thing. Handy as they are, however, pronouns are common stumbling blocks in Greek—even for the grammatically sure of foot. And given the nature of pronouns, it's no wonder.

The main problem with pronouns is that they are inflected, that is, their forms change from one situation to the next. ἐγώ, μου, and με all refer to the same person, but you can't use these words interchangeably as if they were mix-and-match dinner plates. Each form has its proper place. And to put the proper form of the pronoun in its proper place, you need to know something about the different roles that pronouns can play in a sentence. These roles will be the focus of this chapter. First, though, a brief introduction to pronoun usage in general.

The Basics of Pronoun Usage

Understanding pronoun usage presupposes your ability to handle three basic tasks, either consciously or automatically. You must be able to identify the pronoun's *antecedent,* you must be able to recognize what *case* the pronoun is in, and you must know its *person, gender,* and *number.* If all this is familiar to you, you can go directly to our discussion of personal pronouns below. Otherwise it would be a good idea to spend a moment looking over the explanations that follow.

The **antecedent** of a pronoun (sometimes referred to as the **referent**) is the word or words for which the pronoun substitutes. In the sentence "Each man has *his* reward," the antecedent of the pronoun *his* is *man.* In the sentence "John and I have completed *our* travel plans," the pronoun is *our* and the antecedents are *John* and *I.*

Case refers to what function the pronoun is performing in the sentence. The categories are *nominative* (subject), *genitive* (possessor), *dative* (indirect object), and *accusative* (direct object). It must be stressed that the case of a pronoun is independent of its antecedent. Thus, four pronouns in the same sentence can share the same antecedent but still play different roles in the sentence, as in: "Sam wants to make sure that when *he* [subject] arrives next week someone will be at the airport to meet *him* [direct object] to help carry *his* [possessor] suitcases and to hand over the new office keys *to him* [indirect object]." Here all four pronouns have the same antecedent—*Sam*—but each plays a different role in the sentence.

Person is the term used to distinguish the person actually doing the speaking *(first person)* from the person being spoken to *(second person)* and from the person (or thing) being spoken about *(third person).* These categories and their corresponding pronoun forms in English are as follows:

- First person: *I, me, my, mine, we, us, our, ours*
- Second person: *you, your, yours*
- Third person: *he, him, his, she, her, hers, it, its, they, them, their, theirs*

Gender, of course, indicates whether the antecedent is masculine, feminine, or neuter. *Number* refers to whether the antecedent represents one person, place, or thing (singular) or more than one (plural).

Personal Pronouns

The Greek personal pronouns (which, oddly enough, include pronouns applied to things) are:

First Person

	Singular	Plural
N.	ἐγώ	ἡμεῖς
G.	ἐμοῦ or μου	ἡμῶν
D.	ἐμοί or μοι	ἡμῖν
A.	ἐμέ or με	ἡμᾶς

Second Person

	Singular	Plural
N.	σύ	ὑμεῖς
G.	σοῦ or σου	ὑμῶν
D.	σοί or σοι	ὑμῖν
A.	σέ or σε	ὑμᾶς

Third Person

	Singular			Plural		
	M.	**F.**	**N.**	**M.**	**F.**	**N.**
N.	αὐτός	αὐτή	αὐτό	αὐτοί	αὐταί	αὐτά
G.	αὐτοῦ	αὐτῆς	αὐτοῦ	αὐτῶν	αὐτῶν	αὐτῶν
D.	αὐτῷ	αὐτῇ	αὐτῷ	αὐτοῖς	αὐταῖς	αὐτοῖς
A.	αὐτόν	αὐτήν	αὐτό	αὐτούς	αὐτάς	αὐτά

These pronouns are quite common in the New Testament (some 10,779 occurrences), and for good reason. They have three main functions.

First, they relieve boredom. "I see the man and teach the man" is much better expressed as "I see the man and teach *him*." Compare the same sentences in Greek:

- βλέπω τὸν ἄνθρωπον καὶ διδάσκω τὸν ἄνθρωπον.
- βλέπω τὸν ἄνθρωπον καὶ διδάσκω αὐτόν.

The second sentence is preferable as it is less redundant.

Second, personal pronouns give special emphasis. Observe the following sentences:

- διδάσκω καὶ μανθάνεις, I teach and you learn.
- ἐγὼ διδάσκω ἀλλὰ σὺ μανθάνεις, *I* teach but *you* learn.

The separate Greek pronouns ἐγώ and σύ clearly emphasize the subjects of their respective verbs.

Third, the genitive of the personal pronoun is the most common means of showing possession:

- ὁ λόγος μου = the word *of me* = *my* word
- τὸ τέκνον αὐτῆς = the child *of her* = *her* child
- αἱ ἁμαρτίαι αὐτῶν = the sins *of them* = *their* sins

Now, one of the most hallowed principles of grammar is that pronouns agree with their antecedents in gender and number but, as we saw, not necessarily in case. Take, for example, the sentence ἡ γυνὴ ἔρχεται καὶ βλέπω αὐτήν, "The woman is coming and I see *her*." Here the pronoun αὐτήν is feminine and singular, as is its antecedent γυνή. However, αὐτήν is *accusative* (as the object of βλέπω) while γυνή is *nominative* (as the subject of ἔρχεται).

It should be obvious that a personal pronoun matches gender with its antecedent *in its own language*: βλέπω τὸν οἶκον καὶ ἔρχομαι εἰς αὐτόν, "I see the house and go into *it*." In Greek, οἶκον *(house)*, the antecedent of the personal pronoun, is a masculine noun, and so a masculine pronoun (αὐτόν) must be used. In English, however, *house* is neuter, and so we use the pronoun *it*, not *him*. Likewise: γινώσκω τὴν ἀλήθειαν καὶ πιστεύω αὐτήν, "I know the truth and believe *it* [not *her*]."

Αὐτός is used idiomatically in two other ways, which must be carefully distinguished. (1) When it is in the attributive position (i.e., placed between the article and its noun) it is an *adjective* meaning "same": ὁ αὐτὸς ἄνθρωπος, "The *same* man." (2) When it is used in agreement with another substantive it is an *intensive pronoun* meaning *himself, herself,* etc.: αὐτὸς διδάσκει τὸν ὄχλον, "He *himself* teaches the crowd."

Possessive Pronouns

The possessive pronouns of the first and second persons are as follows (there is no third-person possessive pronoun):

ἐμός	*my, mine*
σός	*your, yours*
ἡμέτερος	*our, ours*
ὑμέτερος	*your, yours*

Possessive pronouns are really adjectives of the second and first declensions and, in the manner of all self-respecting Greek adjectives, always agree with their noun in gender, number, and case. Possessive pronouns are generally equivalent to the possessive genitive of the personal pronoun:

- ὁ ἐμὸς κύριος, my Lord = ὁ κύριός μου
- ὁ ἡμέτερος κύριος, our Lord = ὁ κύριος ἡμῶν

Note that when a noun is qualified by a possessive pronoun, it generally has an article in front of it.

Possessive pronouns are used infrequently in the New Testament, possibly with a bit more emphasis than the customary genitive form of the personal pronoun. (In older English *mine* had the same function, as in *"Mine* eyes have seen the glory.")

Reflexive Pronouns

Reflexive pronouns are used when the subject's action "reflects" back upon himself or herself. They are formed by combining the personal pronouns with the oblique cases of αὐτός. (There are no reflexive pronouns in the nominative.) The following examples are all of the accusative case.

ἐμαυτόν	*myself*
σεαυτόν	*yourself*
ἑαυτόν	*himself*
ἑαυτήν	*herself*
ἑαυτό	*itself*
ἑαυτούς	*ourselves, yourselves, themselves*

In the New Testament the genitive form ἑαυτοῦ is sometimes shortened to αὑτοῦ (note the rough breathing). Little more need be said about the reflexive pronouns; after all, they speak for themselves.

Reciprocal Pronouns

The reciprocal pronoun ἀλλήλων (one another) is a reduplication of ἄλλος (another) and occurs only in the oblique cases: ἀγαπῶμεν ἀλλήλους (1 John 4:7), "let us love *one another*." Εἷς τὸν ἕνα can express the same sense: διὸ παρακαλεῖτε ἀλλήλους καὶ οἰκοδομεῖτε εἷς τὸν ἕνα, "therefore, encourage *one another* and build *one another* up" (1 Thess. 5:11). Sometimes the reflexive pronoun is used as a reciprocal: λαλοῦντες ἑαυτοῖς, "speaking *to one another*," not "speaking *to yourselves*" (Eph. 5:19).

Relative Pronouns

The Greek **relative pronoun** ὅς, ἥ, ὅ—so called because it "relates" to someone or something previously mentioned—follows the declension of the definite article. It must agree with its antecedent in gender and number, but its case is determined by its function in its own sentence. A clear understanding of the syntax of the relative is essential.

In the sentence "the voice that I heard was loud," there are two distinct clauses: a principal clause ("the voice was loud") and a subordinate (or relative) clause ("that I heard"). *That* is a relative pronoun, and its antecedent is *voice*. Such a sentence that answers the question "what?" is adjectival in force and is therefore called an "adjectival clause" (see chapter 2).

In the complex sentence "the voice that I heard was loud," the relative pronoun *that* must be feminine singular in Greek because *voice* is feminine singular. But whereas *voice* is the subject of the verb *was* and therefore nominative, *that* is the object of the verb *heard* and therefore accusative. Hence the Greek sentence would read ἡ φωνὴ ἣν ἤκουσα μεγάλη ἦν.

Occasionally the relative agrees, not with the grammatical gender of its antecedent, but with its natural gender: παιδάριον [neuter] . . . ὅς [masculine] ἔχει, "a small boy who has" (John 6:9). In 1 Corinthians 15:10, εἰμὶ ὃ εἰμί, "I am *what* I am," is not a grammatical blooper. By referring to himself with the neuter pronoun, Paul wants to bring out a qualitative force. Εἰμὶ ὃς εἰμί, "I am *who* I am," would have given quite a different twist to Paul's thought.

In certain constructions, the case of the relative pronoun is said to be "attracted" to the case of the antecedent: καὶ τῆς διαθήκης ἧς διέθετο ὁ θεός, "and of the covenant *that* God appointed" (Acts 3:25). The pronoun ἧς has been attracted to the case of διαθήκης even though it is the *object* of the verb διέθετο (the pronoun would normally have been in the *accusative*). Frequently Greek, like English, omits the antecedent altogether where no ambiguity exists: ὃς βλέπει με σωθήσεται, "[he] *who* sees me will be saved."

The relative pronoun is involved in a few idioms: ἀφ᾽ οὗ means *since,* ὃς ἄν means *whoever,* and ὅ ἐστιν can introduce an interpretation: *that is.* Occasionally a superfluous personal pronoun meets us in some relative sentences: γυνή . . . ἧς . . . τὸ θυγάτριον αὐτῆς, "a woman whose little daughter" (Mark 7:25)—literally, "a woman whose *her* little daughter."

Ὅστις is commonly called the **indefinite relative pronoun**. It sometimes means *whoever,* and is practically confined to the nominative: ὅστις, ἥτις, ὅτι (singular); οἵτινες, αἵτινες, ἅτινα (plural). However, there is usually no real difference between the relative pronoun ὅς and the indefinite relative pronoun ὅστις: Ἀβραὰμ ὅστις ἀπέθανεν, "Abraham *who* died" (John 8:53).

Interrogative Pronouns

The usual interrogative in the New Testament (occurring some 500 times) is τίς (masculine and feminine) and τί (neuter). Ποῖος (used only 33 times) normally asks a *qualitative* question ("What sort?"), while πόσος (27 times) asks a *quantitative* question ("How much?"). Τίς and τί are declined according to the pattern of the third declension.

The interrogative may be used as an adjective: τίνα μισθὸν ἔχετε; *"what* reward do you have?"* (Matt. 5:46); or it may be used as a substantive: τίς ὑπέδειξεν ὑμῖν; *"who* warned you?"* (Matt. 3:7).

At times, the neuter interrogative form τί asks "why?": τί ἐποίησας τοῦτο; *"why* did you do this?"*

Indefinite Pronouns

The indefinite pronoun τις is generally translated *someone, anyone,* or *a certain one*. It is distinguished from its close cousin the interrogative pronoun τίς by generally having no accent (though it may be accented in some positions) and by the fact that it cannot stand as the first word in a sentence. Otherwise, these "cousins" are so close so as to require a DNA test to distinguish one from the other (they are declined identically).

The position of τις, when modifying a noun, is generally after the noun: ἄνθρωπός τις [note accentuation], "a *certain* man." In some instances this approaches the English indefinite article and may be translated *a* or *an:* καί τις ἀνήρ, "and *a* man" (Acts 3:2).

In certain passages the adjective πᾶς *(each, every)* seems to be used as a virtual equivalent of τις (see Matt. 5:22: πᾶς ὁ ὀργιζόμενος, *"anyone who is angry")*.

Demonstrative Pronouns

This and *that,* with their plurals *these* and *those,* are called **demonstrative pronouns**. The Greek demonstratives οὗτος *(this)* and ἐκεῖνος *(that)* agree with the nouns they modify in gender, number, and case, just like adjectives. When they qualify a noun, the noun always has the article: οὗτος ὁ ἄνθρωπος or ὁ ἄνθρωπος οὗτος, *"this* man"; ἐκείνη ἡ ἐντολή or ἡ ἐντολὴ ἐκείνη, *"that* commandment."

When οὗτος stands by itself, without any word expressed for it to agree with, it means *this man*. Likewise, αὕτη means *this woman*, τοῦτο means *this thing*, ταῦτα means *these things*, and so on. The forms of ἐκεῖνος can be used the same way (ἐκεῖνος, *that man;* ἐκείνη, *that woman;* ἐκεῖνο, *that thing;* ἐκεῖνα, *those things,* etc.)

Sometimes the demonstrative force of οὗτος and ἐκεῖνος is diminished in the New Testament, especially in the Gospel of John: τοῦτον ἰδὼν ὁ Ἰησοῦς, "when Jesus saw *him*" (John 5:6).

Conclusion

When King Canute ordered the sea to stop rising, it rose anyway. The sea of pronouns is as inexorable. The New Testament contains over 16,500 pronouns. They show up in four-fifths of its verses. If, after reading this chapter, you do not have a better handle on these ubiquitous words, send me an indignant letter and I will print a groveling apology in the next edition of this book (assuming, of course, that there will be a next edition). Meanwhile, the exercises below will depict the spirit of the pronoun in its various manifestations.

For Practice

Put into English the following sentences.

1. οὗτοι οἱ ἄνθρωποι ἀπέθνησκον ἐν τῇ ἐρήμῳ.
2. οὗτος οὖν ἦν μαθητὴς Ἰωάννου.
3. αὗται ἐν τῷ πλοίῳ ἔμενον.
4. αὕτη γὰρ ἦν ἡ ἐντολὴ αὐτοῦ.
5. ἐν ἐκείνῃ τῇ ἡμέρᾳ ἐδόξαζον οἱ ἀπόστολοι τὴν σοφίαν τοῦ κυρίου.
6. αὐτὸς γὰρ σώσει τὸν λαόν.
7. ἔπεμπεν αὐτὴν ἀπὸ τοῦ ἱεροῦ.
8. οὗτοί εἰσιν οἱ οἶκοι αὐτῆς.
9. ἄνθρωπός τις τοῦτο λέγει.
10. ὁ μὴ ὢν μετ᾽ ἐμοῦ κατ᾽ ἐμοῦ ἐστιν.
11. τίς ἐκ τῶν δύο ἐποίησεν τὸ θέλημα τοῦ πατρός;
12. τότε προσῆλθεν αὐτῷ γυνή τις.
13. κύριε, εἰ σὺ θέλεις, κέλευσόν με ἐλθεῖν πρός σε.
14. σὺ μὲν εἶ δοῦλος, ἐγὼ δὲ ἐλεύθερος.
15. ἐβούλοντο ἀκούειν τοὺς λόγους οὓς ἐλάλει ὁ Ἰησοῦς.
16. ἐγώ σε κελεύω ἐξέρχεσθαι ἐκ τῆς οἰκίας.
17. οἱ αὐτοὶ ἄγγελοι ἑτοιμάσουσιν ἑαυτοὺς πορεύεσθαι.
18. ἕξετε ζωὴν ἐν ἑαυτοῖς.
19. πορεύσομαι πρὸς τὴν αὐτὴν οἰκίαν;
20. τί βαπτίζεις εἰ σὺ οὐκ εἶ ὁ Χριστός;

21. εἶπεν αὐτῇ ὁ Ἰησοῦς, Ἐγώ εἰμι ἡ ἀνάστασις καὶ ἡ ζωή.
22. αὕτη ἦν πλήρης ἔργων ἀγαθῶν.
23. τοῦτο τὸ ποτήριον ἡ καινὴ διαθήκη ἐστιν.
24. πῶς δύναταί τις εἰσελθεῖν;
25. τίνι ὁμοιώσω τὴν γενεὰν ταύτην;
26. οὗτός ἐστιν ὁ υἱός μου ὁ ἀγαπητός, ἐν ᾧ εὐδόκησα.
27. κοινωνίαν ἔχομεν μετ᾿ ἀλλήλων.
28. καὶ ἡ κοινωνία δὲ ἡ ἡμετέρα μετὰ τοῦ πατρὸς καὶ μετὰ τοῦ υἱοῦ Ἰησοῦ Χριστοῦ.
29. πᾶσαι αἱ γυναῖκες ἔδωκαν τῷ πατρὶ αὐτῶν τὸ αὐτὸ δῶρον.
30. αὐτὸ τὸ πνεῦμα συνμαρτυρεῖ τῷ πνεύματι ἡμῶν.
31. ὁ ἄνθρωπος ᾧ ἔπεμψα δῶρα ἔρχεται.
32. οὐχ ὑμεῖς με ἐξελέξασθε, ἀλλ᾿ ἐγὼ ἐξελεξάμην ὑμᾶς.
33. ἐγὼ ἠγάπησά σε.
34. τίς ἥμαρτεν, οὗτος ἢ οἱ γονεῖς αὐτοῦ;
35. μέσος ὑμῶν ἔστηκεν ὃν ὑμεῖς οὐκ οἴδατε.
36. παρακαλῶ σε περὶ τοῦ ἐμοῦ τέκνου, ὃν ἐγέννησα ἐν τοῖς δεσμοῖς.
37. κατηργήθητε ἀπὸ Χριστοῦ, οἵτινες ἐν νόμῳ δικαιοῦσθε.
38. ἐν ποίᾳ ἐξουσίᾳ ταῦτα ποιεῖς;
39. πόσους ἄρτους ἔχετε;
40. εἰ υἱὸς εἶ τοῦ θεοῦ, βάλε σεαυτὸν κάτω.
41. εὔχεσθε ὑπὲρ ἀλλήλων.
42. ἡ κρίσις ἡ ἐμὴ δικαία ἐστίν, ὅτι οὐ ζητῶ τὸ θέλημα τὸ ἐμόν.

Key Terms

antecedent
demonstrative pronoun
indefinite pronoun
indefinite relative pronoun
interrogative pronoun
personal pronoun

possessive pronoun
pronoun
reciprocal pronoun
referent
reflexive pronoun
relative pronoun

For Further Reading

Robertson 676–753
Dana and Mantey 122–35
BDF 145–61
Zerwick 63–71
Wallace 315–54

6

Have Mercy on Me, the Sinner

Those Articulate Articles

Greek, as you know, has a definite article—*the*. It lacks, however, an indefinite article, which for some reason was never developed in the history of the language. Indefiniteness may be shown by the absence of the article, or by the indefinite pronoun τις, or by the numeral εἷς with practically the same force as the English *a* or *an:* νομικός τις, "*a* lawyer" (Luke 10:25); εἷς γραμματεύς, "*a* scribe" (Matt. 8:19). When the article is used in Greek, the noun is said to be **articular** or **arthrous** (the Greek word ἄρθρον means "article"); when it is not used, the noun is **anarthrous**.

The Greek article system is not unlike its English counterpart. **Articles** are used to show whether we are referring to things that are known to the speaker and the listener. Think of it as *the = we know which one.* In other words, we use *the* before a noun when our audience knows (or can figure out) which particular person or thing we are talking about. Compare:

- Did you lock *the* car? [The listener knows very well which car is meant.]
- We rented *a* car when we traveled last summer. [The listener does not know which one.]

The listener may know which one we mean because

1. We mentioned it before:

- She has two children: a boy and a girl. *The* boy's fourteen and *the* girl's eight.
- At that point I gave *the* money back to *the* police officer. [The speaker uses *the* because the listener has already heard about the money and the police officer.]

2. We say which one we mean:

- Who's *the* girl over there with John?
- Tell Pat *the* story about John and Mary.
- What did you do with *the* book I lent you?

3. It is clear from the situation which one we mean:

- Could you close *the* door?
- Mary's in *the* kitchen.
- What's *the* time?

4. We are talking about something unique:

- I haven't seen *the* sun for days.
- *The* Japanese are in the news these days.

5. We are describing a common feature of life:

- My wife likes *the* beach, but I prefer *the* mountains.
- I love listening to *the* wind.

6. We are generalizing about the members of a group:

- *The* tiger is in danger of becoming extinct.
- Life would be quieter without *the* telephone.

In many of these examples, *the* behaves very much like the demonstrative pronoun *this*. This is not a coincidence. The Greek definite article was born a demonstrative pronoun, and it has always retained its demonstrative force. In the writings of Homer (ca. 800 B.C.), for example, ὁ, ἡ, τό are the commonest of the demonstrative pronouns: they "demonstrate" or point out individual identity.

It is essential to remember that in Greek, as in Latin (which has no article), a noun may be definite *without the article*. Thus in Matthew 2:3

we have ὁ βασιλεὺς Ἡρῴδης because the emphasis is on the fact of Herod's being king ("Herod *the* king"), while in Luke 1:5 we have ἐν ταῖς ἡμέραις Ἡρῴδου βασιλέως, "in the days of King Herod," emphasizing a certain period of time (the "King Herod days").

When a definite noun lacks the article, stress is being placed on the qualitative aspect of the noun rather than on its identity or particularity. In John 4:27, for example, the disciples were surprised that their Master would talk μετὰ γυναικός, "with *a* woman." Likewise, a qualitative force is seen in the fact that God has spoken ἐν υἱῷ, "in [one whose status is] Son," in contrast to his previous speaking ἐν τοῖς προφήταις, "in *the* prophets" (Heb. 1:1–2). Prepositional phrases usually imply some idea of quality, and the anarthrous noun is common in such phrases: ἐν ἀρχῇ, "in [the] beginning" (John 1:1).

General Uses of the Article

When you are engaged in exegesis, you cannot afford to neglect the article. It is the most frequent word in the New Testament, occurring about twenty thousand times, or once in every seven words. The following are its most important uses.

1. The article can serve to make a substantive particular: ὁ θεός, ἱλάσθητί μοι τῷ ἁμαρτωλῷ, "God have mercy on me, *the* sinner [that I am]" (Luke 18:13). The point of the penitent's prayer is largely missed unless we note the article.
2. The so-called **anaphoric use** of the article has an even more particularizing function. *Anaphora* (the Greeks had a word for everything!) is the reference back to what is known or assumed to be known: "He saw two boats. . . . Getting into one of *the* boats . . ." (Luke 5:2–3). Any noun, once it has been used, can be so defined. Additional examples include:

   - πόθεν οὖν ἔχεις τὸ ὕδωρ τὸ ζῶν; where can you get *the* living water [to which you just referred]? (John 4:11). We may also render this, "Where can you get *this* living water?"
   - τῇ γὰρ χάριτί ἐστε σεσῳσμένοι, for by *the* grace [just spoken of] you are saved (Eph. 2:8). Here the article points back to verse 7, "his [God's] grace." This may also be rendered, "For by *such* grace you are saved."
   - μὴ δύναται ἡ πίστις σῶσαι αὐτόν; can *the* [aforementioned] faith save him? (James 2:14). The rendering "Can faith save him?" (KJV and others) implies that a person is not saved by

faith. But in the first part of the verse James inquires, "What is the benefit, my brothers, if someone says he has faith [πίστιν, anarthrous] but does not have works?" Then he asks, "*Such* faith [ἡ πίστις, arthrous] is not able to save him, is it?" The article with the second use of πίστις designates the particular kind of faith James has in mind—non-works-producing faith. James's point is that genuine faith must express itself in works.

3. The article may be used with proper names such as *Jesus, Paul, John,* etc. Thus, Ἰωάννης may denote any number of individuals, but ὁ Ἰωάννης is a particular individual bearing this name. In general, the article is used with proper names only anaphorically (to indicate that it is the person mentioned previously) or with certain well-known persons. Note Σαῦλος in Acts 8:1, but ὁ Σαῦλος in 9:1; Κορνήλιος in 10:1, but ὑπὸ τοῦ Κορνηλίου in 10:17. Otherwise, the article is generally omitted before proper names.

4. Abstract nouns in Greek are often accompanied by the article when the intent is to give them a particular application, as in 1 Corinthians 11:14: ἡ φύσις αὐτὴ διδάσκει, "[*the*] nature itself teaches." Similarly, νόμος, πνεῦμα, θάνατος, νεκροί, and ἔθνη regularly take the article in the New Testament, though English rarely translates the article in such instances. The article's appearance with abstract nouns is not a universal rule, however: χάριν ἀντὶ χάριτος, "grace in place of grace" (John 1:16).

5. The article may make a substantive representative of a category of items: ὁ ποιμὴν ὁ καλὸς τὴν ψυχὴν αὐτοῦ τίθησιν ὑπὲρ τῶν προβάτων, "*the* good shepherd gives his life for *the* sheep" (John 10:11). This is called the **generic use** of the article. Note also "*the* overseer must be blameless" (1 Tim. 3:2); "*the* foxes have lairs and *the* birds of heaven nests" (Matt. 8:20; Luke 9:58); "*the* rock" and "*the* sand" (Matt. 7:24–26). Sometimes English idiom prefers the indefinite article where Greek has the definite article: ἄξιος γὰρ ὁ ἐργάτης τοῦ μισθοῦ αὐτοῦ, "for *a* worker [is] worthy of his wage" (Luke 10:7).

6. The Greek article is often used where we would use the possessive pronoun in English: Παῦλος ἐκτείνας τὴν χεῖρα, "Paul, reaching out *his* hand" (Acts 26:1); ἀπενίψατο τὰς χεῖρας, "he washed *his* hands" (Matt. 27:24).

7. The article may be used to identify the case of an indeclinable word, or to make a substantive out of another part of speech, or to relate a phrase or clause to some other part of a sentence. Thus ἐκ τούτων τῶν δύο, "of these [*the*] two" (Acts 1:24); ἀπὸ τοῦ νῦν, "from [*the*] now" (Luke 5:10); καὶ οὐχ εὕρισκον τὸ τί ποιήσωσιν,

"and they could not find [*the*] what they might do" (Luke 19:48). This principle may apply to adjectives, adverbs, participles, infinitives, prepositional phrases, clauses, and even entire sentences: τὸ εἰ δύνῃ, πάντα δυνατὰ τῷ πιστεύοντι, "[As for] *the* [remark] 'If you can!'—all things are possible to the one who believes" (Mark 9:23).

8. The original nature of the article as a pronoun can still be seen in the use of the article as a personal pronoun: ὁ δὲ ἐπεῖχεν αὐτοῖς, "and *he* [or *that one*] was observing them" (Acts 3:5). This construction frequently involves a participle: οἱ μὲν οὖν διασπαρέντες διῆλθον εὐαγγελιζόμενοι τὸν λόγον, "then *those who* had been scattered went everywhere preaching the word" (Acts 8:4). The particles μὲν . . . δέ may be coordinated with the article to function like a pronoun: οἱ μὲν ἦσαν . . . οἱ δέ, "*some* were . . . but *others*" (Acts 14:4). A problematic instance is Matthew 28:17: οἱ δὲ ἐδίστασαν. Does this mean "*they* [that is, all of the disciples] doubted," "*some* [of the disciples, but not all] doubted," or "*others* doubted"? The grammar permits all three interpretations.

9. The repetition of the article with some word or phrase that modifies the noun is employed for emphasis. Here the article functions as a mild relative pronoun: ὁ λόγος . . . ὁ τοῦ σταυροῦ, "the word *that* [is] of the cross" (1 Cor. 1:18).

Special Rules for the Article

Two special rules are Colwell's Rule and the Granville Sharp Rule. E. C. **Colwell's Rule** states that a definite predicate nominative, if it precedes the linking verb, occurs without the article approximately 87 percent of the time:[1] καὶ θεὸς ἦν ὁ λόγος, "and *the Word* [subject nominative with the article] was *God* [predicate nominative without the article]" (John 1:1). If the article were also used with θεός, the statement would mean that all of God was expressed in the Word. As it is, the Word is neither "a God" nor equal with the sum total of God. The other persons of the Trinity are implied in θεός. We might paraphrase the entirety of John 1:1 as follows: "In the beginning the Word existed, and the Word was with *the Deity* [τὸν θεόν], and the Word was *Deity* [θεός]." Compare also:

- σὺ εἶ ὁ υἱὸς τοῦ θεοῦ, you are *the* Son of God (John 1:49)
- σὺ βασιλεὺς εἶ τοῦ Ἰσραήλ, you are *the* King [not *a* King] of Israel (John 1:49)

1. See his essay, "A Definite Rule for the Use of the Article in the Greek New Testament," *Journal of Biblical Literature* 52 (1933): 12–21.

- ἐγώ εἰμι τὸ φῶς τοῦ κόσμου, I am *the* light of the world (John 8:12).
- ὅταν ἐν τῷ κόσμῳ ὦ, φῶς εἰμι τοῦ κόσμου, as long as I am in the world, I am *the* light [not *a* light] of the world (John 9:5).

The **Granville Sharp Rule** states that if a single article links two or more singular substantives, the second and subsequent substantives further describe the first.[2] Compare, for example, προσδεχόμενοι τὴν μακαρίαν ἐλπίδα καὶ ἐπιφάνειαν τῆς δόξης τοῦ μεγάλου θεοῦ καὶ σωτῆρος ἡμῶν Ἰησοῦ Χριστοῦ, "looking for the blessed hope and the appearance in glory of our great God and Savior, Jesus Christ" (Titus 2:13). Thus, "the blessed hope" *is* "the appearance in glory," and "our great God and Savior" *is* "Jesus Christ." Note that Sharp's rule does not apply to personal names: τὸν Πέτρον καὶ Ἰάκωβον καὶ Ἰωάννην τὸν ἀδελφὸν αὐτοῦ, "Peter and James and John, his brother" (Matt. 17:1). Nor does it apply to plurals: τινες τῶν γραμματέων καὶ Φαρισαίων, "some of the scribes and Pharisees" (Matt. 12:38).

Conclusion

Every category of New Testament language abounds in depths of truth that captivate the heart. In this chapter we noticed truth revealed even in the Greek articles.

It is vital to bear in mind that we cannot determine the English translation by the presence or absence of the article in Greek. Sometimes we will use the article in English when it is not used in Greek, and sometimes the force of the Greek article may best be rendered by an anarthrous English noun. The best rule in this matter, once again, is common sense.

For Practice

Put into English the following sentences.

1. ἀλλ᾽ εἰσὶν ἐξ ὑμῶν τινες οἳ οὐ πιστεύουσιν.
2. ἡ δὲ Μάρθα περιεσπᾶτο περὶ πολλὴν διακονίαν.
3. ἀλλ᾽ ἡ τελεία ἀγάπη ἔξω βάλλει τὸν φόβον.
4. πᾶς ὁ πιστεύων ἐπ᾽ αὐτῷ οὐ καταισχυνθήσεται.
5. μακάριοι οἱ ἐλεήμονες, ὅτι αὐτοὶ ἐλεηθήσονται.

---

2. See his *Remarks on the Uses of the Definite Article in the Greek Text of the New Testament* (London: Vernor and Hood, 1798).

6. ἡ γὰρ αὔριον μεριμνήσει ἑαυτῆς.
7. ὁ λόγος γὰρ ὁ τοῦ σταυροῦ τοῖς μὲν ἀπολλυμένοις μωρία ἐστίν.
8. κατανοήσατε τὸν ἀπόστολον καὶ ἀρχιερέα τῆς ὁμολογίας ἡμῶν.
9. ὑμεῖς δὲ τὸν ἅγιον καὶ δίκαιον ἠρνήσασθε.
10. μακάριος ὁ γρηγορῶν καὶ τηρῶν τὰ ἱμάτια αὐτοῦ.
11. μακάριοι οἱ πεινῶντες καὶ διψῶντες τὴν δικαιοσύνην.
12. καὶ αὕτη ἐστιν ἡ μαρτυρία τοῦ Ἰωάννου.
13. καὶ ἐπλήσθη πνεύματος ἁγίου ἡ Ἐλισάβετ.
14. Ἀβραὰμ ἐγέννησεν τὸν Ἰσαάκ, Ἰσαὰκ δὲ ἐγέννησεν τὸν Ἰακώβ.
15. χάριτι δὲ θεοῦ εἰμι ὅ εἰμι.
16. κύριον τὸν θεόν σου προσκυνήσεις.
17. οὕτως λαμψάτω τὸ φῶς ὑμῶν ἔμπροσθεν τῶν ἀνθρώπων.
18. ὁ κλέπτης οὐκ ἔρχεται εἰ μὴ ἵνα κλέψῃ καὶ θύσῃ καὶ ἀπολέσῃ.
19. βασιλεύς εἰμι τῶν Ἰουδαίων.
20. σὺ οὖν εἶ ὁ υἱὸς τοῦ θεοῦ;
21. ἐγὼ Παῦλος ἔγραψα τῇ ἐμῇ χειρί.
22. μάρτυς γάρ μού ἐστιν ὁ θεός.
23. πρὸ τοῦ δὲ ἐλθεῖν τὴν πίστιν ὑπὸ νόμον ἐφρουρούμεθα.
24. καὶ ἐθαύμαζον ἐν τῷ χρονίζειν ἐν τῷ ναῷ αὐτόν.
25. καὶ προσελθὼν εἷς γραμματεὺς εἶπεν αὐτῷ, Διδάσκαλε, ἀκολουθήσω σοι.

Key Terms

anaphoric use of the article
anarthrous
arthrous
article

articular
Colwell's Rule
generic use of the article
Granville Sharp Rule

For Further Reading

Robertson 754–96
Dana and Mantey 135–53
BDF 131–45
Zerwick 53–62
Wallace 206–90

7

Up, Up, and Away

Those Preposterous Prepositions

Prepositions often raise eyebrows. Years ago a preposition that ended a sentence was punishable by the student's equivalent of the death penalty—rewriting a composition. Winston Churchill, I am told, once had a speech criticized because he broke this rule. "This is the sort of English up with which I will not put," was his classic rejoinder. His statement, of course, is clearly more awkward than its alternative, which ends with a preposition (two, in fact): "This is the sort of English which I will not put up with." Let's face it: it's sometimes hard to avoid using a preposition to end a sentence with.

The General Use of Prepositions

By definition, a preposition is a small word that occurs before a noun phrase and combines with it to make a *prepositional phrase*. The term **preposition** itself reflects this "pre-position" or "position before" noun phrases. A **postposition** is just like a preposition, except that it follows its noun phrase. Generally a given language has either prepositions or postpositions. Here are some examples from a postpositional language, Panjabi, spoken by about 20 million people in northwest India and Pakistan (Panjabi is an Indo-European language, and therefore a distant relative of both English and Greek):

- *janvari nu* = January in = in January
- *ghar to* = house from = from the house
- *manje ute* = bed on = on the bed

Both prepositions and postpositions typically express relationships in time or space, or between things and events. Examples of English prepositions are *to, in, at, by, for, with, under, over, below, after,* and *since.* In English, there are some two-word (and even three-word) sequences that act just like single-word prepositions (e.g., *instead of, next to, in front of*). From the point of view of grammar, these sequences behave like single words and are best regarded as being prepositions. In any language there are relatively few prepositions compared to some of the other parts of speech, such as nouns and verbs.

A preposition can form a **prepositional phrase** with a following noun phrase. The following are all prepositional phrases: *for me, under the couch, since the January storm, before the Second World War,* and *with his father.* When a prepositional phrase is used to modify a noun, it forms a new, larger, noun phrase with the noun:

- the only one *for me*
- the book *under the couch*
- the period *since the January storm*
- a conference *before the Second World War*
- the boy *with his father*

Prepositional phrases that modify nouns are often equivalent to longer relative clauses with the verb *be,* as in

- the book *that was under the couch*
- the boy *who was with his father*

When prepositional phrases modify verbs or whole clauses, they are often interchangeable with adverbs, as in these examples:

- it crawled *under the couch* = it crawled *there*
- she was born *before the Second World War* = she was born *then*

A prepositional phrase can also be used as a predicate, that is, with the verb *be* or another linking verb such as *remain* or *become:*

- your book is *under the couch*
- Paul remained *with his father*

In Greek, prepositions tend to cause trouble because some of them govern as many as three cases. In English, however, all prepositions take the objective (accusative) case.

Proper Prepositions

The Greek prepositions were originally adverbs (and are still so used when compounded with verbs). Greek has eighteen so-called **proper prepositions**—"proper" in that they may be used both independently and in composition with verbs:

- proper prepositions used with *one case* only: (1) genitive: ἀντί, ἀπό, ἐκ, πρό, (2) dative: ἐν, σύν, (3) accusative: ἀνά, εἰς
- proper prepositions used with *two cases* (genitive and accusative): διά, κατά, μετά, περί, ὑπέρ, ὑπό
- proper prepositions used with *three cases* (genitive, dative, accusative): ἐπί, παρά, πρός

The remaining proper preposition, ἀμφί, though used independently in Classical Greek, occurs in the New Testament only in composition with verbs.

These eighteen prepositions are constantly being prefixed to verbs, as in ἐκβάλλω, "I throw out," from βάλλω, "I throw." The following are the principal meanings of the proper prepositions when compounded with verbs:

- ἀμφί = *around* (ἀμφιβάλλω)
- ἀνά = *up* (ἀναβαίνω); *up, again, back* (ἀναζάω)
- ἀντί = *against* (ἀντιλέγω); *instead* (cf. the noun ἀντίλυτρον)
- ἀπό = *away, off* (ἀπολύω); often intensive (ἀποκτείνω = "I kill *off*")
- διά = *through* (διαβαίνω); often intensive (διαμαρτύρομαι = "I *solemnly* declare")
- εἰς = *into* (εἰσάγω)
- ἐκ = *out* (ἐκβάλλω)
- ἐν = *in* (ἐγκρύπτω); *into* (ἐμβαίνω)
- ἐπί = *upon* (ἐπιβαίνω)
- κατά = *against* (κατακρίνω); *down* (καταφέρω); often intensive (καταδιώκω = "I hunt *down*")
- μετά = *with* (μετέχω); often denotes change (μετανοέω)
- παρά = *beside* (παραλαμβάνω); *at* (πάρειμι)
- περί = *around* (περιβάλλω); *to excess* (περιεργάζομαι)
- πρό = *before* (προγινώσκω); *forth* (προβάλλω)

- πρός = *towards* (προσέρχομαι); *to* (προσάγω)
- σύν = *with* (συγχαίρω)
- ὑπέρ = *over* (ὑπεραίρομαι); *beyond* (ὑπερβάλλω)
- ὑπό = *under* (ὑποδέω); denotes submission (ὑποτάσσω)

Note that phonological changes must be allowed for in compound verbs: ἐκ becomes ἐξ before a vowel (e.g., ἐκ + ἄγω = ἐξάγω); ἐν and σύν become ἐγ and συγ before gutturals (e.g., ἐν + κρύπτω = ἐγκρύπτω); and σύν becomes συλ before λ and συμ before a labial or μ (e.g., συν + μαρτύρομαι = συμμαρτύρομαι).

A Tale of Twelve Mice
(Greek Prepositions Illustrated)

ὑπέρ + acc.

ἐπί + gen.

κατά + gen.

διά + gen.

περί + acc.

ἐν + dat.

εἰς + acc.

ὑπό + acc.

κατά + acc.   ἐκ + gen.

παρά + acc.

ἀπό + gen.

πρός + acc.

Art by Roger Lau '80

Improper Prepositions

Unlike the above, the so-called **improper prepositions** cannot be compounded with verbs. They are really adverbs, and nearly all govern the genitive case. Below is a list of the most common improper prepositions.

- ἅμα, together with
- ἄνευ, without
- ἄχρι(ς), until
- ἐγγύς, near
- ἔμπροσθεν, before
- ἐναντίον, in front of, against, opposite
- ἕνεκα or ἕνεκεν, for the sake of
- ἐνώπιον, before, in the presence of
- ἔξω, outside
- ἐπάνω, above
- ἔσω, within
- ἕως, as far as
- μέσον, in the midst of
- μεταξύ, between
- μέχρι(ς), until
- ὀπίσω, ὄπισθεν, behind, after
- ὀψέ, at the end of
- πλήν, except
- πλησίον, near; παραπλήσιον, very near
- ὑπερέκεινα, beyond
- χάριν, for the sake of
- χωρίς, apart from

The Character of Prepositions

The Greek prepositions have really very little to say for themselves that hasn't already been said as plainly as the lexicons and reference grammars could possibly have said it (see the postscript). Here I should simply like to say a few words about the character of New Testament prepositions before you begin to interpret them.

Due to Semitic influence, the New Testament use of prepositions has several distinctive characteristics, including

- an increase in the frequency of prepositional phrases
- the frequency of a prepositional phrase with εἰς after linking verbs
- the use of ἐν to express instrumentality, accompaniment, and causality

- the frequent use of ἔμπροσθεν reflecting the Hebrew *liphnê*
- the repetition of a preposition with each noun connected by καί to highlight the distinction between them.

As a result of these distinctives, you should be aware of several pitfalls in examining prepositional usage in the New Testament:

- Be careful not to insist on Classical Greek distinctions. For example, in Koine Greek both εἰς and ἐν can express the idea of location; hence, there is no need to insist on direction or movement for εἰς in John 1:18 (*"into* the bosom of the Father"). Other examples of interchange include ὑπέρ and περί (e.g., περὶ πολλῶν in Matt. 26:28 is ὑπὲρ πολλῶν in Mark 14:24); ἀπό and ἐκ (cf. Matt. 7:16 with Luke 6:44); ἀπό and παρά (cf. John 13:3 with John 16:27, 28); and πρός and εἰς (cf. Mark 5:38f with Mark 11:1).
- Always make allowance for a writer's style. The New Testament writers often used different prepositions in successive phrases simply to avoid repetition or to vary their style (note, for example, that both ἀπό and ἐκ are used with τοῦ οὐρανοῦ in John 6:38, 42).
- On the other hand, one must assume that the New Testament writers chose their prepositions with care. For example, in the last clause of the Lord's Prayer (Matt. 6:13b) it is relevant to observe that ἀπό, not ἐκ, follows ῥῦσαι. In the New Testament ἀπό is used with persons, while ἐκ denotes deliverance from non-personal enemies. Hence it is probable that τοῦ πονηροῦ means "the evil one" rather than "evil."
- Because a preposition tends to be repeated before each noun in a series of nouns joined by καί, sometimes the non-use of a second or third preposition in New Testament Greek may be significant, indicating that the writer regarded the terms in one list as belonging together in concept or reality. The phrase ἐξ ὕδατος καὶ πνεύματος in John 3:5 is a possible example: "water and Spirit" together form a single means of regeneration. Similarly, the fact that "God our Father" and "the Lord Jesus Christ" are joined by a single preposition (ἀπό) in the Pauline salutations suggests that the apostle viewed the Father and the Son as a joint source of "grace and peace" (cf. 1 Cor. 1:3).

Conclusion

To sum up, in any discussion of the New Testament prepositions two opposite dangers are to be avoided: to treat them as synonymous everywhere they appear, and to insist on too rigid a distinction between them. As with so many other things in life, it helps to be a (passionate) moderate.

For Practice

Put into English the following sentences.

1. περιπατῶν δὲ παρὰ τὴν θάλασσαν εἶδεν δύο ἀδελφούς.
2. εἰσέλθετε διὰ τῆς στενῆς πύλης.
3. ἐπειδὴ γὰρ δι᾿ ἀνθρώπου ὁ θάνατος, καὶ δι᾿ ἀνθρώπου ἀνάστασις νεκρῶν.
4. καὶ χρηματισθέντες κατ᾿ ὄναρ μὴ ἀνακάμψαι πρὸς Ἡρώδην, δι᾿ ἄλλης ὁδοῦ ἀνεχώρησαν εἰς τὴν χώραν αὐτῶν.
5. οὐ περὶ τούτων δὲ ἐρωτῶ μόνον.
6. ἔπειτα μετὰ ἔτη τρία ἀνῆλθον εἰς Ἱεροσόλυμα.
7. καθ᾿ ἡμέραν πρὸς ὑμᾶς ἐκαθεζόμην διδάσκων ἐν τῷ ἱερῷ.
8. εἰ ὁ θεὸς ὑπὲρ ἡμῶν, τίς καθ᾿ ἡμῶν;
9. μὴ κρίνετε κατ᾿ ὄψιν, ἀλλὰ τὴν δικαίαν κρίσιν κρίνετε.
10. καὶ ἀπολαβόμενος αὐτὸν ἀπὸ τοῦ ὄχλου κατ᾿ ἰδίαν, ἔβαλε τοὺς δακτύλους αὐτοῦ εἰς τὰ ὦτα αὐτοῦ.
11. καὶ ὁ πεσὼν ἐπὶ τὸν λίθον τοῦτον συνθλασθήσεται.
12. ἐξεπλήσσοντο οἱ ὄχλοι ἐπὶ τῇ διδαχῇ αὐτοῦ.
13. εἴ τις ὑμᾶς εὐαγγελίζεται παρ᾿ ὃ παρελάβετε, ἀνάθεμα ἔστω.
14. καὶ γὰρ ἐγὼ ἄνθρωπός εἰμι ὑπὸ ἐξουσίαν, ἔχων ὑπ᾿ ἐμαυτὸν στρατιώτας.
15. δικαιωθέντες οὖν ἐκ πίστεως εἰρήνην ἔχομεν πρὸς τὸν θεὸν διὰ τοῦ κυρίου Ἰησοῦ Χριστοῦ.

Key Terms

improper prepositions   prepositional phrase
postposition   proper prepositions
preposition

For Further Reading

Robertson 553–649
Dana and Mantey 96–115
BDF 110–25
Zerwick 27–135
Wallace 355–89

PART **3**

Rho, Rho, Rho Your Boat

The Greek Verb System

8

Tense Times with Verbs (1)

An Overview of Greek Inflections

Tommy: I ain't going.

Teacher: Don't say "ain't." Say, "I am not going, you are not going, he is not going."

Tommy: Ain't nobody going?

Or maybe you heard the one about the man who went on trial for having pulled a woman down the street by her hair. When the judge asked the arresting officer "Was she drugged?" the policeman replied, "Yes sir, a whole block!"

Both jokes rely on the fact that verbs in English are crazy, fraught with puzzling unpredictability. Some verbs form their past tense by adding *-d, -ed,* or *-t,* as in *walk, walked; bend, bent.* Others go back in time through an internal vowel change—*begin, began; sing, sang.* Another cluster adds *-d* or *-t* and undergoes an internal vowel change—*lose, lost; bring, brought.* And still others don't change at all—*set, set; put, put.*

Greek verbs are no less confusing than their English cousins. If you don't agree, try forming the past tense of *eat* (ἐσθίω) or of *bring* (φέρω) without your breath quickening or your eyes glazing. The slopes of this mountainous linguistic terrain are filled with the dead and dying—people who were conjugated, parsed, and inflected into oblivion.

Yet you can't get away from verbs. Without a verb, you cannot have a complete sentence. So you might say that verbs are the most important part of a sentence.

How the Greek Verb Works

We've already seen that a Greek noun can be divided into two elements: the stem and the ending. It's the same with the verb, except that you can also add something to the front of the stem as well as change the appearance of the stem itself. All of these changes are called **inflections**. So you begin with the stem and separate it from its inflections. Then you examine the inflections to find all the information they contain.

Because inflections contain so much vital information, they are the key to understanding Greek verbs. Inflections ask and answer the following five questions:

1. Who is doing the action?
2. How many are doing the action?
3. Is the subject doing the action or is it being done to the subject?
4. How does the speaker view the kind of action?
5. How does the speaker view the relation of the action to reality?

Sometimes inflections ask a sixth question: When does the action happen? Grammarians call these six areas (1) person, (2) number, (3) voice, (4) aspect, (5) mood, and (6) time (or tense). Thus, every time you encounter a Greek verb you must seek to answer five, and sometimes six, questions.

Let's take a closer look at these six questions.

Person

Person indicates the relation of the subject to the action.

- If the subject is represented as speaking, the verb is in the **first person**: ἀκούω, I hear (ἀκού = hear; -ω = I).
- If the subject is being spoken to, the verb is in the **second person**: ἀκούεις, you hear (ἀκού = hear; -εις = you).
- If the subject is being spoken about, the verb is in the **third person**: ἀκούει, he hears (ἀκού = hear; -ει = he).

Notice where the subject is: in the ending. Greek does not add an independent pronoun to indicate the subject. When an independent pronoun is used it emphasizes the subject: ἐγὼ ἀκούω, "*I* hear."

In short, to the first question, "What is its person?" there are three possible answers: first person, second person, or third person.

Number

If the assertion made by the verb concerns more than one person, the verb is in the plural: ἀκούομεν, "we hear"; ἀκούετε, "you [all] hear"; ἀκούουσι, "they hear."

Notice that modern English makes no distinction of number in the second person, so that *you hear* can be either singular or plural. Some dialects of English get around this by having a special second-person plural form, such as *youse* in parts of Scotland, *y'all* in the southeastern United States, and *you guys* or *you people* in much of North America. If these forms are used regularly, then presumably *you* becomes by default the second person singular.

Greek, however, distinguishes between second person singular and second person plural. For example, in John 4:20 the Samaritan woman says to Jesus, "Our ancestors worshiped on this mountain, but *you* say the place where people should worship is in Jerusalem." Here *you* cannot refer to Jesus alone because it is plural in the Greek. The Greek means something like, *"You Jews* say. . . ."* Another example is Jesus' statement to Nicodemus in John 3:7: "Don't be astonished that I said to *you* [singular], *'You* [plural] must be born again.'" Obviously Nicodemus wasn't the only person who needed a new birth. So always observe the number in reading Greek.

Concord in number refers to the normal pattern of singular subject with singular verb and plural subject with plural verb. The only point on which Greek differs from English is in its rule that a nominative plural subject, if it is *neuter,* may be followed by a singular verb: τὰ ὀνόματά ἐστιν ταῦτα, "the names are [literally, *is*] these" (Matt. 10:2). But when emphasis is laid on the individuality of the persons or things described by the neuter plural, the rule does not apply: ἐπαναστήσονται τέκνα, "children will rise up" (Matt. 10:21). On the other hand, collective nouns (in the singular) sometimes take a plural verb: ἤρξαντο ἅπαν τὸ πλῆθος . . . αἰνεῖν τὸν θεόν, "all the crowd [singular] began [plural] . . . to praise God" (Luke 19:37). An exception to the rule of concord is known as a ***constructio ad sensum***—a "construction according to sense" rather than according to strict grammatical concord.

Hence, to the second question, "What is its number?" there are only two possible answers: singular or plural.

Voice

Inflections also indicate whether you are doing the action or if it is being done to you. When the subject is represented as *producing* the action of the verb, the verb is in the **active voice**. When the subject is represented as *receiving* the action of the verb, it is said to be in the **passive voice**. Thus, ἀκούω means "I hear," and ἀκούομαι means "I am being heard." However, Greek has a third way of indicating the relation of the subject to the verb. This is called the **middle voice**, since traditionally it has been put "in the middle":

| Active Voice | Middle Voice | Passive Voice |
| I hear | I hear myself | I am being heard |

I have translated the middle voice as if it had a reflexive meaning. But the reflexive sense of the middle voice was only the way it got started. By the time the New Testament appeared on the scene, this reflexive meaning had almost completely disappeared. The sense of the middle voice is really like underlining the subject or putting it in italics: *I* hear.

In summary, then, the active voice stresses the subject as producing the action. It represents the simplest use of the verb and may be either a **simple active** ("but God *knows* your hearts," Luke 16:15) or a **causative active** ("*he causes* his sun to shine," Matt. 5:45).

The passive voice denotes the subject as receiving the action and may be either a **simple passive** ("*you will be baptized* with the Holy Spirit," Acts 1:5) or a **permissive passive** ("why not *allow yourselves to be defrauded?*" 1 Cor. 6:7). When the passive voice is used, the **agent** or producer of the action may be expressed. **Primary agency** (or **personal agency**) is expressed by ὑπό plus the genitive case, while **secondary agency** (or **intermediate agency**) uses διά plus the genitive: ἵνα πληρωθῇ τὸ ῥηθὲν ὑπὸ κυρίου διὰ τοῦ προφήτου, "in order that the things spoken *by* the Lord *through* the prophet might be fulfilled" (Matt. 1:22). Here the primary agent is the Lord, while the secondary or intermediate agent is the prophet. **Instrumental agency** (or **impersonal agency**) is expressed by the dative case with or without ἐν: ἐν αἵματι πάντα καθαρίζεται, "all things are cleansed *by* blood" (Heb. 9:22). Frequently, however, agency is not expressed: πεπλήρωται ὁ καιρός, "the time is fulfilled" (Mark 1:15). When the unspecified agent of the action is God, the construction is sometimes called the "divine passive": παρακληθήσονται, "*they will be comforted* [by God]" (Matt. 5:4). In other instances, the implicit agent is more generic: οὐ δύναται λυθῆναι ἡ γραφή, "the Scripture *cannot be broken* [by anyone]" (John 10:35).

The middle voice stresses the agent of the action, that is, the grammatical subject. Just how the agent is being emphasized is not indicated by the middle voice but must be deduced from the context. When this is done, the following uses of the middle voice in Greek can be distinguished:

- The **direct middle** has a reflexive force: ἀπελθὼν ἀπήγξατο, "having gone out, *he hanged himself*" (Matt. 27:5). This sense of the middle, as we have seen, is rare in the New Testament. It is almost always taken over by the active voice in the verb plus a reflexive pronoun (*himself, herself,* etc.). See also Mark 14:54 (ἦν . . . θερμαινόμενος, "[Peter] *was warming himself*"); Acts 12:21 (ἐνδυσάμενος, "[Herod] *clothed himself*"); and Revelation 3:18 (περιβάλῃ, "[that] *you might clothe yourself*").

- The **intensive middle** emphasizes the part taken by the subject in the action of the verb: αἰωνίαν λύτρωσιν εὑράμενος, "*he himself secured* eternal redemption" (Heb. 9:12). Here the subject acts *for* himself or herself or in his or her *own interest.* Apart from the deponent middle (see below), this is the most common use of the middle voice in the New Testament. See also Luke 10:42 (ἐξελέξατο, "[Mary] *has chosen for herself*"); Acts 5:2 (ἐνοσφίσατο, "*he kept back for himself* [some of the price]"); and James 1:21 (δέξασθε, "*receive for yourselves* [the implanted word]").

- The **reciprocal middle** represents an interchange of action between or among the members of a plural subject: συνεβουλεύσαντο, "*they conferred with one another*" (Matt. 26:4). See also John 9:22 (συνετέθειντο, "[the Jews] *had agreed with one another*"). In the New Testament this idiom has largely been replaced by an active verb with the reciprocal pronoun ἀλλήλων.

Many verbs in Greek, alas, do not have any active voice endings. The meaning is active, to be sure, but the ending is either in the middle or the passive voice. These are called **deponent verbs** since they are thought to have deposited their active forms in moth balls, thus "putting them aside" (from the Latin verb *depono,* I put aside). Compare the following:

- πιστεύω (I believe) is a regular verb with an active suffix (-ω).
- ἔρχομαι (I come) is a deponent verb with a middle/passive suffix (-μαι).

The most common deponent verbs in the New Testament are ἀποκρίνομαι (I answer), ἄρχομαι (I begin), βούλομαι (I wish), γίνομαι (I become), δέομαι (I pray), δέχομαι (I receive), δύναμαι (I can), ἐργάζομαι (I work), ἔρχομαι (I come), εὐαγγελίζομαι (I preach the gospel), πορεύομαι (I go), προσεύχομαι (I pray), and χαρίζομαι (I forgive). Of course, the only way you can tell whether or not a verb is deponent is from the Greek lexicon. Deponent verbs will end in -μαι.

Thus, to the third question, "What is its voice?" there are three possible answers: active, middle, or passive. In the New Testament, the active voice is far and away the most common, with 20,697 occurrences. The passive has only 3,933 occurrences, and the middle has even fewer—a mere 3,500.

Aspect

Greek speakers could regard action in three fundamentally different ways. This is called **aspect**. Most often an action was regarded as simple or undefined. The common term for this kind of action is **aoristic aspect** (from the Greek adjective ἀόριστος, "undefined"). Aoristic aspect was used when the Greek writer didn't want you to pay any attention to the duration or completion of the action. Think of it as a snapshot: "Jesus *wept*," "Christ *died* for our sins," "God so *loved* the world," and so on. The action itself could have taken years, but that's not the point. What the writer is saying is, "The duration or completion of the action is not important, so just ignore it. What *is* important is that it happened." Thus ἐβασίλευσεν (Rom. 5:14) covers the period from Adam to Moses in which death "reigned"; ἐκρύβη (Heb. 11:23) covers a period of three months in which Moses "was hidden"; οἰκοδομήθη (John 2:20) covers a period of forty-six years during which the temple "was built"; and μαθητεύσατε (Matt. 28:19) covers the entire church age in which Christians are to "make disciples." So never jump to the conclusion that aoristic aspect is instantaneous. The action *may* be instantaneous, but only the context or the meaning of the verb can tell you that.

The Greeks could also regard an action as a process or as habitual. The common term for this sort of action is **imperfective aspect** (from the Latin adjective *imperfectivum*, "not completed"). If you think of aoristic aspect as a snapshot, imperfective aspect would be a motion picture.

Finally, the Greeks could regard an action as a completed event with ensuing results, in which case the aspect is said to be **perfective** (from the Latin adjective *perfectivum*, "completed").

You can describe an action in any of these three ways. For example, you might talk about studying Greek as follows:

- Aoristic Aspect: I studied Greek [in seminary].
- Imperfective Aspect: I was studying Greek [when the phone rang].
- Perfective Aspect: I have studied Greek [and still remember it].

Notice that aoristic aspect is the least distinctive in terms of kind of action. Nevertheless, many preachers and commentators view it as special in some quasi-esoteric way and therefore greatly exaggerate its significance. Doubtless you have heard, at one time or another, someone wax eloquent about the virtues of the aorist tense: "Paul's use of the aorist in Romans 12:1 means that we are to present our bodies *once and for all* to God as a living sacrifice!" Actually, aoristic aspect is about as mundane a category as you can find. And it never means "once and for all," no matter who tells you that it does. As someone has put it, "Its special meaning is that it does not have a special meaning." Period.

So to the fourth question, "What is its aspect?" there are three possibilities: aoristic, imperfective, or perfective.

Mood

If aspect indicates the speaker's attitude toward the kind of action, **mood** indicates the speaker's attitude toward the kind of reality behind his or her statement. Maybe the action really did happen, or maybe it could have happened, or maybe someone wished that it would happen, or maybe someone commanded it to happen.

Greek uses four moods to express these attitudes:

- Indicative (used 15,618 times):   I *shut* the door.
- Subjunctive (used 1,858 times):   I asked that he *shut* the door.
- Optative (used 68 times):   I wish he would *shut* the door.
- Imperative (used 1,631 times):   *Shut* the door.

Actually, these four categories can be boiled down to two essential viewpoints with regard to mood: that which is *actual* (the indicative), and that which is *potential* (the subjunctive, optative, and imperative). Thus, *mood is the feature of a verb that a speaker uses to portray whether he or she has an actuality or a potentiality in mind.* Only the indicative mood has temporal relations. The element of time is entirely absent from the other moods. Thus, verbal aspect tends to be more significant in the potential moods than in the indicative mood.

In studying the Greek moods, remember that mood has to do only with the *manner* in which a statement is made, not necessarily with the *truth* of the statement. Most lies, exaggerations, and fictional accounts are told in the *indicative* mood. ("Tom Cruise is the greatest athlete alive today" is in the indicative mood, but the statement has no objective correspondence to reality.)

Indicative Mood

The **indicative mood** is the simplest and most common mood in the New Testament. It is the unmarked or "default" mood form, used when there is no special reason for employing another mood. You use it for making statements and asking questions: "You are listening to me" and "Are you listening to me?" Because the indicative makes an affirmation it is often called the **mood of reality**.

There are three main uses of the indicative.

- The **declarative indicative** states a simple statement of fact in past, present, or future: διὰ τοῦτο παρεκλήθημεν, for this reason *we were called* (1 Thess. 3:7).
- The **imperatival indicative** expresses a command: ἀγαπήσεις τὸν πλησίον σου, *you shall love* your neighbor (James 2:8). The same command can be given in English as *"Love* your neighbor."
- The **interrogative indicative** is used in a simple question that expects an answer: πιστεύεις τοῦτο, *do you believe* this? (John 11:26).

Note that Greek can indicate whether the anticipated answer to a question is yes or no. With οὐ, an *affirmative* answer is expected: οὐ πιστεύεις ὅτι ἐγὼ ἐν τῷ πατρὶ καὶ ὁ πατὴρ ἐν ἐμοί ἐστιν, "You believe, don't you, that I am in the Father and the Father is in me?" (John 14:10). The anticipated answer is, "Of course!" With μή, a *negative* answer is expected: μὴ κατὰ ἄνθρωπον ταῦτα λαλῶ; "I don't speak these things according to man, do I?" (1 Cor. 9:8). Here the anticipated answer is, "Of course not!" Many queries, however, are *open questions,* giving no grammatical indication whether a positive or negative answer is expected: ἐξ ἔργων νόμου τὸ πνεῦμα ἐλάβετε ἢ ἐξ ἀκοῆς πίστεως, "Did you receive the Spirit by the works of the Law or by the hearing of faith?" (Gal. 3:2). Sometimes a question does not ask for information but is used simply to draw attention to something, in which case it is called a *rhetorical question* ("Do you know what time it is?" = "You're late!").

Subjunctive Mood

Of the moods of potentiality, the **subjunctive mood** is the most frequent, and you can hardly read a half-dozen verses in the New Testament before encountering it. The subjunctive is customarily used to express a hope or desire: "I'm calling so that you might know what happened." Grammarians call it the **mood of probability** because it represents the action as uncertain but probable. As such, it is closely related to the future indicative. The future, however, indicates what *will* take place, whereas the subjunctive indicates what *may* take place.

The different tenses in the subjunctive have no time reference; they differ only according to kind of action—the aorist refers to undefined action, the present to continuous, repeated, or habitual action. The principal uses of the subjunctive are as follows. (Note that while subjunctives may be used as the main verb in a sentence, they more frequently function as a dependent verb in a clause, describing some relationship to the main verb.)

- The **hortatory subjunctive** uses the first person plural to urge others to join with the speaker in a course of action and requires the words *let us* in translation: ἀγαπῶμεν ἀλλήλους, *let us love one another* (1 John 4:7); φάγωμεν καὶ πίωμεν, αὔριον γὰρ ἀποθνήσκομεν, *let us eat and drink, for tomorrow we die* (1 Cor. 15:32). These could also be rendered *"We should love . . ."* and *"We should eat and drink. . . ."*

- The **subjunctive of prohibition** involves μή plus the aorist subjunctive and is used to forbid an action as a whole or, in some instances, to forbid the initiation of an action: μὴ νομίσητε ὅτι ἦλθον καταλῦσαι τὸν νόμον, *don't think* that I came to destroy the Law [or possibly] *don't begin to think* that I came to destroy the Law (Matt. 5:17); μὴ μοιχεύσῃς, μὴ φονεύσῃς, *don't ever commit adultery, don't ever murder* (Luke 18:20). (When the prohibition is against doing something already begun, the construction is μή with the present *imperative;* see below.)

- The **deliberative subjunctive** is used in questions that call for a decision about the proper course of action: τὸν βασιλέα ὑμῶν σταυρώσω; *should I crucify your king?* (John 19:15).

- The **subjunctive of emphatic negation** involves the aorist subjunctive with the double negative οὐ μή and is used to strongly deny that something will happen: οὐ μὴ ἀπόλωνται εἰς τὸν αἰῶνα, *they shall certainly not perish* at any time (John 10:28).

- The **final subjunctive** is used with ἵνα or ὅπως to indicate the purpose of an action: πάντα ὑπομένω διὰ τοὺς ἐκλεκτούς, ἵνα καὶ αὐτοὶ σωτηρίας τύχωσιν, I endure all things for the sake of the elect *in order that they too might obtain* salvation (2 Tim. 2:10).

- The **content subjunctive** introduces the content of what is desired or thought, or it may express indirectly the words of a speaker: πληρώσατέ μου τὴν χαρὰν ἵνα τὸ αὐτὸ φρονῆτε, Fulfill my joy *by thinking* the same thing (Phil. 2:2); οὐκ ἐρωτῶ ἵνα ἄρῃς αὐτοὺς ἐκ τοῦ κόσμου, I do not ask *that you take them* out of the world (John 17:15).

Optative Mood

The **optative mood**, which was already in its death throes when the apostle Paul was learning Greek, is even more removed from reality than the subjunctive. If the subjunctive is the mood of *probability*, the optative is the **mood of possibility**, employed when the speaker wants to portray an action as possible. Its use is confined to the present and aorist tenses.

There are two basic functions of the optative.

- The most common is to express a wish or a prayer, as in Paul's famous declaration μὴ γένοιτο, *may it never be!* (Rom. 3:4). This is called the **voluntative optative**.
- The **potential optative** is used to express what would or might be possible: πῶς γὰρ ἂν δυναίμην ἐὰν μή τις ὁδηγήσει με, *how could I, unless someone guides me?* (Acts 8:31).

Imperative Mood

The **imperative mood** is the **mood of volition** or **intention**. It is used for giving commands: *"Listen* to me!" The distinction between aorist and present is the same as in the subjunctive: the aorist expresses undefined action, the present expresses linear or habitual action.

There are four main uses of the imperative mood.

- The **imperative of command** makes a direct demand upon the will of another: πάντοτε χαίρετε, always *rejoice* (1 Thess. 5:16); φεύγετε τὴν πορνείαν, *flee* immorality (1 Cor. 6:18).
- The **imperative of prohibition** is used with the negative adverb μή and the present imperative to forbid habitual action or, in some instances, to stop an action already in progress: μὴ πλανᾶσθε, *don't be deceived* [or possibly] *stop being deceived* (1 Cor. 6:9); μὴ γογγύζετε, *don't grumble* [or possibly] *stop grumbling* (John 6:43). Note that only the context can tell whether the action is already under way. (When the prohibition is against doing something *not* already begun, the construction is μή with the aorist *subjunctive;* see above.)
- The **imperative of entreaty** expresses a request made by a person of subordinate status to a person of superior status and is often best expressed by using the word *please* in translation: βοήθησον ἡμῖν, *please help us* (Mark 9:22).
- The **imperative of permission** is used to give consent to the desire of another: ὑπάγετε, *you may go* (Matt. 8:32).

Occasionally a command in Greek uses the third person imperative: ὁ καυχώμενος ἐν κυρίῳ καυχάσθω, *let* the one who boasts *boast* in the Lord (1 Cor. 1:31). Although you must use *let* in translating third person imperatives, the force of the imperative is not an option. The Greek is telling you, "The one who boasts *must boast* in the Lord!"

In the imperative mood there is often a contrast between aoristic and imperfective aspect. A good example of this is seen in the two versions of the Lord's Prayer.

- δὸς ἡμῖν σήμερον, *"give* us today" (Matt. 6:11), uses the *aorist* imperative δός. In keeping with its aspectual force, the aorist expresses a summary command in which the action is viewed as a whole, without any regard to its continuance or frequency.
- δίδου ἡμῖν τὸ καθ᾽ ἡμέραν, *"keep on giving* us day after day" (Luke 11:3), uses the *present* imperative δίδου. Here the present tense portrays an ongoing process.

There is one more thing you need to know about aspect in the imperative mood, and that is the distinction between imperatives involving *general precepts* and those involving *specific commands*. General precepts are broad moral regulations and normally involve the *present* tense: τίμα τὸν πατέρα καὶ τὴν μητέρα, *"honor* your father and your mother" (Matt. 15:4). Specific commands are orders or requests for action to be done in a particular instance and tend to use the *aorist* tense: ἀπαγγείλατε Ἰωάννῃ ἃ εἴδετε καὶ ἠκούσατε, *"report* to John what you have seen and heard" (Luke 7:22). Sometimes both concepts are involved in the same passage: ἄρατε ταῦτα ἐντεῦθεν, μὴ ποιεῖτε τὸν οἶκον τοῦ πατρός μου οἶκον ἐμπορίου, *"Take* these things away [*aorist* imperative, suggesting an urgent, specific command]; *do not continue to make* my Father's house a house of merchandise [*present* imperative, suggesting a continuous or habitual action]" (John 2:16).

Thus, to the fifth question, "What is its mood?" there are four possible answers: indicative, subjunctive, optative, or imperative. Only if the mood is indicative do you ask the sixth and final question: "What is its time?" *Always stop with question five unless your answer to that question is the indicative mood.* This is because time in Greek is decidedly secondary to the kind of action being described.

Time (Tense)

When the indicative mood *is* used, either past, present, or future must be expressed. Any one of the three aspects discussed above may be placed in any one of these three time frames. Let's combine them here:

	Past	**Present**	**Future**
Aoristic	Aorist tense	Present tense	Future tense
	I heard	I hear	I will hear
Imperfective	Imperfect tense	Present tense	Future tense
	I was hearing	I am hearing	I will be hearing
Perfective	Pluperfect tense	Perfect tense	Future perfect tense
	I had heard	I have heard	I will have heard

In past time, the three aspects are expressed by what grammarians call the **aorist tense** (I heard), **imperfect tense** (I was hearing), and **pluperfect tense** (I had heard). In present time, the **present tense** must make do for both aoristic aspect (I hear) and imperfective aspect (I am hearing); perfective aspect is expressed by the **perfect tense** (I have heard). Finally, in future time, the **future tense** handles both aoristic (I will hear) and imperfective (I will be hearing) aspects, while the **future perfect tense** (I will have heard) handles perfective aspect.

Conclusion

To summarize what we have said to this point: you should ask every Greek verb five, and sometimes six, questions:

1. What is its person? Your options are: first person, second person, or third person.
2. What is its number? Your options are: singular or plural.
3. What is its voice? Your options are: active, middle, or passive.
4. What is its aspect? Your options are: aoristic, imperfective, or perfective.
5. What is its mood? Your options are: indicative, subjunctive, optative, or imperative. *Only* if your answer to this question is "indicative" should you ask the next question.
6. What is its time (tense)? Your options are: past, present, or future.

Key Terms

active voice	concord
agent	*constructio ad sensum*
aorist tense	content subjunctive
aoristic aspect	declarative indicative
aspect	deliberative subjunctive
causative active	deponent verb

direct middle
final subjunctive
first person
future perfect tense
future tense
hortatory subjunctive
imperatival indicative
imperative mood
imperative of command
imperative of entreaty
imperative of permission
imperative of prohibition
imperfect tense
imperfective aspect
impersonal agency
indicative mood
inflection
instrumental agency
intensive middle
intermediate agency
interrogative indicative
middle voice
mood
mood of intention
mood of possibility
mood of probability
mood of reality

mood of volition
number
optative mood
passive voice
perfect tense
perfective aspect
permissive passive
person
personal agency
pluperfect tense
potential optative
present tense
primary agency
reciprocal middle
second person
secondary agency
simple active
simple passive
subjunctive mood
subjunctive of emphatic
  negation
subjunctive of prohibition
tense
third person
time
voice
voluntative optative

For Further Reading

Robertson 797–950
Dana and Mantey 155–208
BDF 161–96
Zerwick 72–124
Wallace 390–586

9

Tense Times with Verbs (2)

Interpreting the Greek Tenses

The interpretation of the Greek tenses calls for a closer look at the indicative mood, since time of action is not involved in the other moods.

Action in Past Time

Aorist Tense

The word *aorist*, as we have seen, means "unlimited" or "undefined." It was given to this tense by grammarians to denote that the action spoken of is to be regarded simply as an event, without any regard to the time in which it occurs or the length of time during which it has been going on. However, this statement must be qualified with respect to the indicative mood. Here the aorist has an augment and is generally used of events that are spoken of as occurring in *past* time. It is therefore the most suitable Greek tense to translate the English simple past tense ("I heard," "I believed," "I was saved"). Thus, the aorist indicative is a past-tense form, but it is the augment, the sign of past time, that makes it so, not the term *aorist*.

A given aorist-tense form may have any one of three points of emphasis: it may accent the beginning of the action, it may accent the conclusion of the action, or it may look at the whole action without any emphasis on its beginning or conclusion.

- If it stresses the beginning of the action it is an **ingressive aorist**: ὁ λόγος σὰρξ ἐγένετο, the Word *became* flesh (John 1:14); ἐπτώχευσεν, [Christ] *became poor* (2 Cor. 8:9); ἐδάκρυσεν ὁ Ἰησοῦς, Jesus *burst into tears* (John 11:35).
- If the emphasis is on the end of the action, rather than its beginning, it is an **effective aorist**: ἐγὼ γὰρ ἔμαθον ἐν οἷς εἰμι αὐτάρκης εἶναι, for *I have learned* to be content in whatever circumstances I am (Phil. 4:11).
- If the action involved is viewed as a whole, a **constative aorist** is used: ἐπέμεινα πρὸς αὐτὸν ἡμέρας δεκαπέντε, *I remained* with him for fifteen days (Gal. 1:18).

These emphases, it must be noted, are concessions to the English point of view. The aorist itself simply regards the action as an event. The aorist also has several "special" uses.

- The **gnomic aorist** is used to express a universal or timeless truth: ἐδικαιώθη ἡ σοφία ἀπὸ πάντων τῶν τέκνων αὐτῆς, wisdom *is vindicated* by all her children (Luke 7:35).
- The **epistolary aorist** is used by writers when they put themselves in the position of their readers and look back on the time of writing as a past event: ἐγὼ Παῦλος ἔγραψα τῇ ἐμῇ χειρί, I, Paul, *write* [this] with my own hand (Philem. 19).
- The **dramatic aorist** describes something that has just happened, the effect of which is felt in the present: οὗτός ἐστιν ὁ υἱός μου ὁ ἀγαπητός, ἐν ᾧ εὐδόκησα, you are my beloved Son, in whom *I am well pleased* (Matt. 3:17).

It should be obvious that all these distinctions are determined by context alone. There is absolutely no formal difference between a *constative aorist* and a *dramatic aorist,* and many times even the context is not fully conclusive, as the disagreements among commentators prove.

Imperfect Tense

Strictly speaking, the **imperfect tense** views the action as in progress. It is represented by the English past continuous forms ("I was teaching," "I used to go"). But a simple past tense ("I taught," "I went") may sometimes be a sufficient translation for a Greek imperfect tense.

If the aorist tells the story, the imperfect helps you to see the flow of the action. There is a variety of ways in which it may do this.

- The **progressive imperfect** emphasizes the duration of the action: τί ὅτι ἐζητεῖτέ με, why *were you looking* for me? (Luke 2:49).
- The **iterative imperfect** emphasizes the repetition of the action: ἤρχοντο πρὸς αὐτὸν καὶ ἔλεγον, Χαῖρε, ὁ βασιλεὺς τῶν Ἰουδαίων, [people] *kept coming* to him and *kept saying*, "Hail, king of the Jews" (John 19:3).
- The **tendential imperfect** presents the action as having been attempted but not accomplished: ὁ ... Ἰωάννης διεκώλυεν αὐτόν, John *was trying to prevent* him (Matt. 3:14).
- The **inceptive imperfect** emphasizes the beginning of the action: εἰσελθὼν εἰς τὴν συναγωγὴν ἐδίδασκεν, when he entered the synagogue, *he began to teach* (Mark 1:21). This usage is very frequent in the New Testament.

It is important to distinguish between imperfect and aorist and to note that Greek prefers to use the aorist in narrative unless there is a need to emphasize that an action is in progress. So, for example, in Luke 17:27 four imperfects describe the life of Noah's day: they were eating (ἤσθιον), they were drinking (ἔπινον), they were marrying (ἐγάμουν), and they were giving in marriage (ἐγαμίζοντο). The other verbs in the verse are all aorists: "entered," "came," "destroyed." Another interesting example is found in Matthew 1:24–25: "[Joseph] did as the angel of the Lord had told him, and he took [Mary] as his wife; yet he was not knowing her until she brought forth her firstborn son." The imperfect οὐκ ἐγινώσκεν αὐτήν, "was not knowing her," shows that Joseph lived in continence with the virgin until after the birth of the Savior.

Pluperfect Tense

The **pluperfect tense** indicates a past state resulting from an action prior to it. The state continued up to some point in the past, at which time it presumably ceased (otherwise the perfect tense would have been used). The pluperfect was never widely used, even in Classical Greek, but it does occur a few times in the New Testament. The uses of the pluperfect are identical to those of the perfect tense (see below).

Action in Present Time

Present Tense

The **present tense** normally expresses action as being in process in present time, that is, at the time of speaking, though it may also be used of the past and of the future. Inasmuch as the indicative mood has no distinct tense for aoristic aspect in present time, the present tense is used to perform that function. However, the Greek present tense generally corresponds more clearly to the English continuous present ("I am teaching") than to the simple present ("I teach"). The present tense has several prominent uses.

- The **descriptive present** describes the action as currently taking place: κύριε, σῶσον, ἀπολλύμεθα, Lord, save [us]! *We are drowning!* (Matt. 8:25).
- The **progressive present** describes an action begun in the past as continuing into the present: τοσαῦτα ἔτη δουλεύω σοι, all these years *I have been serving* you (Luke 15:29).
- The **iterative present** depicts an action that is repeated at certain intervals: ὑπωπιάζω μου τὸ σῶμα καὶ δουλαγωγῶ, *I repeatedly beat* my body and *subdue* [it] (1 Cor. 9:27).
- The **tendential present** indicates an action being attempted or proposed but that has not actually taken place: κύριε, σύ μου νίπτεις τοὺς πόδας, Lord, *are you going to wash* my feet? (John 13:6).
- The **historical present** describes a past event as though it were actually taking place: λέγουσιν αὐτῷ περὶ αὐτῆς, *they spoke* to him about her (Mark 1:30). Here the present is a pictorial tense, displaying the action vividly before our eyes. In English we often use the historical present when recounting personal experiences ("then he *says* to me").
- The **futuristic present** describes what is going to take place in the future as though it were already occurring: ὑπάγω καὶ ἔρχομαι πρὸς ὑμᾶς, *I will go away* and *will come* to you (John 14:28). English has a similar idiom: "he *is coming* tomorrow."
- The **aoristic present** expresses the action as a simple event without any reference to its progress: τέκνον, ἀφίενταί σου αἱ ἁμαρτίαι, child, your sins *are forgiven* (Mark 2:5).

Perfect Tense

The **perfect tense** describes an action as completed at the time of writing or speaking. While dealing with the past to some extent, the perfect tense is primarily concerned with present time. An action has occurred in the past whose results are still apparent. Thus τέθνηκε (the perfect of ἀποθνῇσκω) does not mean "he died" but "he is *now* dead." Similarly, γέγραφα (the perfect of γράφω) means "[it is *there* on paper, because] I wrote [it]."

There is no exact English equivalent to the Greek perfect. The so-called English perfect, formed by the auxiliary verb *have*, is the nearest equivalent that can be given, but it will not always serve to translate a Greek perfect. The perfect tense has three main uses.

- The **intensive perfect** expresses a present state resulting from a past action: οὕτως γέγραπται παθεῖν τὸν Χριστόν, thus *it is written that the Christ should suffer* (Luke 24:46).
- The **consummative perfect** emphasizes the completed action: ἡ πίστις σου σέσωκέν σε, your faith *has made you well* (Mark 10:52).
- The **dramatic perfect** is used to bring a past event vividly into the present: Ἰωάννης μαρτυρεῖ περὶ αὐτοῦ καὶ κέκραγεν, John testifies about him and *cries out* (John 1:15).

Action in Future Time

Future Tense

The future tense sometimes expresses aoristic aspect ("*I will preach from Romans next year*"), sometimes imperfective ("*I will be preaching every Sunday*"), with the aoristic aspect being the more frequent. Notice that the element of time is more obvious in the future tense than in the other tenses.

- The **predictive future** affirms that an action will take place or that a state will come into being: αὐτὸς ὑμᾶς βαπτίσει, *he himself will baptize* you (Matt. 3:11).
- The **progressive future** emphasizes the progress of a future action: ἀλλὰ καὶ χαρήσομαι, indeed, *I will keep on rejoicing* (Phil. 1:18).
- The **imperatival future** can be used in place of the imperative mood to express a command: καλήσεις τὸ ὄνομα αὐτοῦ Ἰησοῦν, *you will call* his name Jesus, [that is,] *you are to call* his name Jesus (Matt. 1:21).
- The **deliberative future** is used in real or rhetorical questions to consult the judgment of another person: τίνι . . . ὁμοιώσω τὴν γενεὰν ταύτην, to what *shall I compare* this generation? (Matt. 11:16).

Again I must warn you that only the context can determine the difference between predictive, progressive, and other futures. The fact that scholars often engage in long and inconclusive debates over certain uses should be sufficient proof that the differences are not always clear-cut. Correct methodology treats the whole clause first and then allows the context to determine the nuance of the tense that is used.

Future Perfect Tense

The future perfect tense was never widely used in Koine Greek and is almost extinct in the New Testament. The verb εἰδήσουσιν (Heb. 8:11) is the only certain instance, and it has lost its perfective force (it means "they will know").

Periphrastic Tenses

In Greek, as in English, tenses are sometimes formed by a form of the verb *be* (usually εἰμί) and a participle: ἦν . . . διδάσκων αὐτούς, "*he was teaching* them" (Matt. 7:29). These are called **periphrastic tenses** because they are expressed in a "roundabout" way (from περί, "around," and φράζω, "I express"). The most common periphrastic tenses in the New Testament are the periphrastic imperfect, the periphrastic perfect, and the periphrastic pluperfect. The periphrastic construction is often used to highlight verbal aspect.

- The **periphrastic imperfect** is formed by the imperfect of εἰμί and the present participle: καὶ ἦν προάγων αὐτοὺς ὁ Ἰησοῦς, and Jesus *was going* before them (Mark 10:32).
- The **periphrastic pluperfect** is formed by the imperfect of εἰμί and the perfect participle: καὶ ἦν ὁ Ἰωάννης ἐνδεδυμένος τρίχας καμήλου, and John *was clothed* with camel's hair (Mark 1:6).
- The **periphrastic perfect** is formed by the present of εἰμί and the perfect participle: ὁ λαὸς καταλιθάσει ἡμᾶς, πεπεισμένος γάρ ἐστιν Ἰωάννην προφήτην εἶναι, the people will stone us, for *they are persuaded* that John is a prophet (Luke 20:6).

Principal Parts

You have now encountered all the tenses of the Greek verb. At the end of the book you will find a chart setting out all the moods and tenses of the verb λύω ("I loose"). This verb is perfectly regular in the formation of its tenses, but many Greek verbs form one or more of their tenses in an irregular way. This is regrettable, but there is nothing you (or I) can do about it. In order to identify the various parts of a given verb, grammarians have invented a convention called **principal parts**, which are the present active, future active, aorist active, perfect active, perfect middle/passive, and aorist passive forms of the verb. The principal parts of "I loose" are:

1. λύω (I loose)
2. λύσω (I will loose)
3. ἔλυσα (I loosed)
4. λέλυκα (I have loosed)
5. λέλυμαι (I have loosed/I have been loosed)
6. ἐλύθην (I was loosed)

A list of the main verbs you are likely to need in reading the New Testament is given in appendix 2. You should eventually learn the whole list by heart. This is not as difficult as it may seem if you work on a few at a time, say five a day.

Conclusion

You have come to it—the end of your overview of Greek inflections. Many other details could have been given, but at this stage of the game you need to know those details as much as the Boston Celtics need elevator shoes.

You must, however, keep in mind that interpretations that lean too heavily on subtle nuances of Greek verbs are seldom worth considering. For instance, it is all too easy to "over-exegete" verbal aspect. "Do not believe every spirit" (1 John 4:1) uses an imperative of prohibition in the present tense. Does this imply that John wants his readers to *stop* being deceived? Possibly, but this grammatical construction doesn't always forbid an action in progress. Once again, it is the context, and the context alone, that is determinative.

Your challenge is to use your understanding of Greek verbs *as one part* of your ongoing study of the most important book in the world. And you will enhance your ministry if you wear this knowledge with grace and humility.

For Practice

Put into English the following sentences.

1. κρίνει ὁ κύριος τὰς ψυχὰς τῶν ἀνθρώπων.
2. ἡ ἐκκλησία πιστή ἐστιν.
3. τέκνα ἀγαπητά ἐσμεν τοῦ θεοῦ.
4. ὁ πρῶτός ἐστιν ἔσχατος, καὶ ὁ ἔσχατος πρῶτος.
5. ἅγιος εἶ, κύριε.
6. καλοῦμεν τοὺς ἑτέρους νεανίας.
7. ἐκηρύσσομεν τὸ εὐαγγέλιον τῷ λαῷ.
8. ἔπεμπεν ὁ θεὸς τοὺς ἀγγέλους αὐτοῦ εἰς τὸν κόσμον.
9. ὁ Ἰησοῦς αὐτὸς οὐκ ἐβάπτιζεν ἀλλὰ οἱ μαθηταὶ αὐτοῦ.
10. ἐπέμπεσθε ὑπὸ τῶν διδασκαλῶν πρὸς ἕτερον ὄχλον.
11. μετὰ ταῦτα οἱ τελῶναι ἐδιδάσκοντο ὑπὸ πρεσβυτέρων ἐν τῇ ἐκκλησίᾳ.
12. ἐπορευόμεθα μετὰ τῶν μαθητῶν πρὸς τὴν θάλλασαν.
13. οἱ πρεσβύτεροι ἕξουσι τὰ πρόβατα ἃ σώζεται ἀπὸ τῶν ἐχθρῶν.
14. προφητεύσεις τῷ λαῷ τούτῳ καὶ ὑπακούσουσίν σοι.
15. κρύψομεν τὸ παιδίον ἐν τῇ οἰκίᾳ;
16. ἁγιάσατε ἑαυτούς, ἐγγίζει γὰρ ἡ ἡμέρα τοῦ κυρίου.
17. ἡ εἰρήνη κατοικείτω τὰς καρδίας ὑμῶν.
18. ἔπεμψας τοὺς τελώνας ἀγοράσαι τὰ ἱμάτια.
19. εἶπεν ὅτι εἶδε τὰ πλοῖα.
20. ἐν τούτῳ γινώσκομεν τὴν ἀγάπην τοῦ θεοῦ, ὅτι ἔπεμψεν τὸν υἱὸν αὐτοῦ τὸν ἀγαπητὸν εἰς τὸν κόσμον.
21. ἔγνωμεν ὅτι πολλὰ ἔμαθον οἱ μαθηταὶ ἀπὸ τῶν ἀποστόλων.
22. ὅτε δὲ οἱ στρατιῶται ἦλθον εἰς τὴν οἰκίαν ἀπήγγειλαν ὅτι ἀπέστειλεν αὐτοὺς ὁ Πέτρος.
23. ὁ δὲ Ἰησοῦς εἶπεν τῷ παραλυτικῷ, Ἔγειρε ἆρον τὴν κλίνην σου καὶ ὕπαγε εἰς τὸν οἶκόν σου, ὡς δὲ ἤκουσεν ταῦτα ἦρεν τὴν κλίνην καὶ ὑπῆγεν.
24. ὁ προφήτης εἶπεν ὅτι πάντα δυνατά ἐστι παρὰ τῷ θεῷ.
25. ἤχθη ὁ Ἰησοῦς ὑπὸ τοῦ πνεύματος εἰς τὰ ὄρη πειρασθῆναι ὑπὸ τοῦ διαβόλου.
26. τῇ γὰρ χάριτι ἐσώθημεν διὰ θελήματος θεοῦ.
27. καὶ ὅτε ἐξεβλήθη τὸ δαιμόνιον ἐθαύμαζεν ὁ ὄχλος, ἔλεγον δὲ πολλοὶ ὅτι ταῦτα τὰ τέρατα οὐκ ἦσαν τοῦ θεοῦ.
28. ἐκλήθητε ἄφρονες ὑπὸ τῶν σοφῶν τοῦ αἰῶνος τούτου.
29. πεπληρώκατε τὴν Ἰερουσαλὴμ τῆς διδαχῆς ὑμῶν.
30. ὁ θεὸς εἴρηκε τοῦτο διὰ στόματος πάντων τῶν προφητῶν.
31. ἦλθεν ἵνα μαρτυρήσῃ περὶ τοῦ φωτός.

32. ὃς ἂν πιστεύσῃ εἰς τὸ ὄνομα τοῦ κυρίου σωθήσεται.
33. λέγωμεν ἄρα ποιήσωμεν τὰ κακά, ἵνα ἔλθῃ τὰ ἀγαθά;
34. καλῶς ἀθετεῖτε τὴν ἐντολὴν τοῦ θεοῦ, ἵνα τὴν παράδοσιν ὑμῶν τηρήσητε.
35. μὴ κρίνετε ἵνα μὴ κριθῆτε.
36. μὴ φόβου, ἀλλὰ λάλει καὶ μὴ σιωπήσῃς.

Key Terms

aorist tense
aoristic present
constative aorist
consummative perfect
deliberative future
descriptive present
dramatic aorist
dramatic perfect
effective aorist
epistolary aorist
future perfect tense
future tense
futuristic present
gnomic aorist
historical present
imperatival future
imperfect tense
inceptive imperfect

ingressive aorist
intensive perfect
iterative imperfect
iterative present
perfect tense
periphrastic imperfect
periphrastic perfect
periphrastic pluperfect
periphrastic tenses
pluperfect tense
predictive future
present tense
principal parts
progressive future
progressive imperfect
progressive present
tendential imperfect
tendential present

For Further Reading

See the references at the end of chapter 8.

10

To Be or Not to Be

The Infinitive

Hamlet pondered the question, "To be or not to be?" To study or not to study the infinitive is not open to question.

Nobody is really sure which part of speech infinitives belong to, even today. The Greek infinitives seem to have started life as the dative form of nouns made from verbs. Eventually, the infinitive was voted a new status: it was now considered a mood of the verb on a par with the indicative, subjunctive, optative, and imperative. What that means, essentially, is that infinitives usually get listed with verbs instead of with nouns.

In English, the preposition *to* before the bare form of the verb marks it as an infinitive. This preposition is not a part of the infinitive but is a relic of the dative case of the verbal noun in Old English. The infinitive forms of verbs (along with their helping preposition *to*) are italicized in the following sentences:

- Do you want *to go* with me?
- I prefer *to stay* at home.
- *To tell* the truth, I haven't gotten ready yet.
- *To be* so late embarrasses me.

The preposition *to* may be omitted after certain verbs such as *can, may, let,* and others ("can you *go* with me?").

113

The forms of infinitives do not convey person or number, though they do have tense in both English and Greek:

- *To love* is good (present infinitive)
- 'Tis better *to have loved* (perfect infinitive)

However, because Greek does not use gerunds, the infinitive must do double duty:

- *Loving* is fun

Here *loving* is a gerund; Greek would use the infinitive.

In many languages the infinitive is marked by a special suffix. Italian infinitives, for example, all end in *-are, -ire,* or *-ere,* French infinitives all end in *-er, -ir,* or *-re,* and German infinitives all end in *-en*. In Greek, infinitives are marked by the following suffixes:

- -ειν in the present active.
- -αι in the aorist active.
- -ναι in the perfect and aorist passive.
- -σθαι elsewhere.

Nature of the Greek Infinitive

But down to brass (or bronze) tacks. To understand how Greek infinitives operate, you must be acquainted with certain rules of the road.

- As a substantive, the infinitive may be used in any case except the vocative. It is always indeclinable, always in the singular number, and always in the neuter gender. The infinitive may be qualified by adjectives and accompanied by a preposition.
- The infinitive may be used with or without the article; the article, if used, is always declined and always neuter (τό, τοῦ, τῷ). The neuter article is used because the infinitive is an absolute concept. Hence in English it is perhaps better to think of the infinitive as "the action of . . ." rather than as "to . . .": τὸ ἐλθεῖν, "the action of going."
- As a verb, the infinitive has both tense and voice. The force of the voice may not be as prominent as in the indicative mood, but it is always present. The tense will always be timeless, and the aspect will either be aoristic (undefined action), imperfective (continuous action), or perfective (completed action). As a verb, the infini-

tive may also govern cases, as a finite verb does, and be qualified by adverbs. The negative used with the infinitive is almost always μή instead of οὐ.

- Both the substantival and the verbal force of the infinitive should be observed in interpretation. Both will be present, although one will predominate. A good example is Philippians 1:21: τὸ ζῆν Χριστός, "to go on living [is] Christ." "To go on living" is the *subject* of the clause (this brings out the substantival idea). It is in the *present* tense, emphasizing a *continuous* relationship with Christ (bringing out the verbal idea)—a momentous point often neglected in English translations.

- Normally, an infinitive's subject will be the same subject as that of the main verb. Note, for example, 1 Thessalonians 3:5: ἔπεμψα εἰς τὸ γνῶναι τὴν πίστιν ὑμῶν. This may be translated as "I sent [him] in order *to know* about your faith" or as "I sent [him] so that *I would know* about your faith." When an infinitive takes a distinct subject, however, that subject will be in the *accusative* case. In 1 Thessalonians 1:8, ἡμᾶς (accusative plural) is the subject of ἔχειν in the clause ὥστε μὴ χρείαν ἔχειν ἡμᾶς λαλεῖν τι, "As a result, *we* do not have a need to say anything."

- When two elements are found in the accusative, it is sometimes difficult to tell which element is the subject of the infinitive. A well-known example is Philippians 1:7: διὰ τὸ ἔχειν με ἐν τῇ καρδίᾳ ὑμᾶς. Does Paul mean "because I have you in my heart" or "because you have me in your heart"? The Greek permits either interpretation (με and ὑμᾶς are the words in question). If you're wondering how such confusion is possible, try the following finger exercise. Make a circle with the fingers on your left hand by touching the tip of your index finger to the tip of your thumb. Now poke your head through the circle. If you unsuccessfully tried to fit your head through the small digital ring, you took the phrase "poke your head" to mean that your head was the poker. But the phrase "poke your head" has a second, opposite meaning: that the head is the pokee. So, if you had raised your left hand with the circle of fingers up close to your forehead and poked your right index finger through the circle until it touched your forehead, you would have successfully completed the exercise. Fortunately, a rule of grammar helps us in translating Philippians 1:7: when two items are found in the accusative case, the subject usually *precedes* the object. Hence the translation "I have you in my heart" is probably correct.

- Finally, many Greek infinitives may be translated as English infinitives: λαβεῖν, "to take," φιλεῖν, "to love," and so on. On other occasions they may be rendered as participles or as indicative verbs.

Main Uses of the Infinitive

Now that you've encountered the genius of the infinitive, it's time to feast your eyes on a potpourri of infinitival expressions that grace the table of the Greek language.

1. **Complementary Infinitive**. This is the most common usage by far. An infinitive may be used with such verbs as *be able, want, wish, begin, try, seek, avoid, ask, allow, hinder, owe,* and so on. The infinitive complements or completes the thought begun by that verb.

- καὶ τίς δύναται σωθῆναι, then who is able *to be saved*? (Mark 10:26)
- εἴ τις θέλει πρῶτος εἶναι, ἔσται πάντων ἔσχατος, if anyone wants *to be* first, he will be last of all (Mark 9:35)

2. **Epexegetical Infinitive**. The infinitive may further explain adjectives, nouns, and pronouns. In this way it differs from the complementary infinitive, which complements verbs.

- ὃ ἐπήγγελται δυνατός ἐστιν καὶ ποιῆσαι, what he promised, he is able also *to do* [the infinitive ποιῆσαι complements the predicate adjective δυνατός] (Rom. 4:21)
- τοῦτο γάρ ἐστιν θέλημα τοῦ θεοῦ, ὁ ἁγιασμὸς ὑμῶν, ἀπέχεσθαι ὑμᾶς ἀπὸ τῆς πορνείας, for this is the will of God, your sanctification, for you *to abstain* from immorality [the infinitive ἀπέχεσθαι complements the noun ἁγιασμός] (1 Thess. 4:3)

3. **Infinitive of Indirect Discourse**. Greek has several ways of turning a direct statement into an indirect statement. The usual idiom involves a ὅτι clause: ἐνόμισαν ὅτι πλεῖον λήμψονται, "they thought that they would receive more" (Matt. 20:10). (The direct statement would have been, "We will receive more.") Sometimes, however, the infinitive is used to express indirect discourse:

- αὐτὸς ἐπηρώτα αὐτούς, ὑμεῖς δὲ τίνα με λέγετε εἶναι, he asked them, "Who do you say that *I am*?" (Mark 8:29)
- καὶ ἔρχονται Σαδδουκαῖοι πρὸς αὐτόν, οἵτινες λέγουσιν ἀνάστασιν μὴ εἶναι, and Sadducees, who say *there is* no resurrection, came to him (Mark 12:18)

As the preceding examples illustrate, the infinitive may function as the object of a verb expressing thought or verbal communication in a statement, question, command, or prohibition. Verbs commonly employed in this function include λέγω, νομίζω, and δοκέω. The subject will be in the accusative case, and the infinitive may need to be translated with a participle or indicative verb. The infinitive always appears without a definite article.

- ὁ λέγων ἐν αὐτῷ μένειν, the one who says that *he abides* in him [the actual statement was ἐν αὐτῷ μένω] (1 John 2:6)
- ὥστε ὁ δοκῶν ἑστάναι βλεπέτω μὴ πέσῃ, so that the one who thinks *he stands,* let him see to it that he does not fall [the actual statement was ἵστημι] (1 Cor. 10:12)

4. **Substantival Infinitive**. Here the infinitive acts like a noun, functioning as the subject or object of a verb.

- τὸ ζῆν Χριστὸς καὶ τὸ ἀποθανεῖν κέρδος, *to go on living* [is] Christ, and *to die* [is] gain (Phil. 1:21)
- ἔλαχε τοῦ θυμιᾶσαι, he obtained by lot *the privilege of making the sacrifice* (Luke 1:9)

5. **Infinitive of Time**. The infinitive may follow a preposition (πρὸ τοῦ or πρίν or πρὶν ἤ = *before;* ἐν τῷ = *while;* μετὰ τό = *after;* ἕως τοῦ = *until*), and is normally translated like an indicative verb or a participle. Below are examples of each category. Note that the subjects of the infinitive are in the *accusative* case.

- πρὶν ἤ συνελθεῖν αὐτοὺς εὑρέθη ἐν γαστρὶ ἔχουσα, *before they came together,* she was found to be pregnant (Matt. 1:18)
- καὶ ἐν τῷ σπείρειν αὐτὸν ἃ μὲν ἔπεσεν παρὰ τὴν ὁδόν, and *while he sowed,* some [seeds] fell beside the road (Matt. 13:4)
- ἀλλὰ μετὰ τὸ ἐγερθῆναί με προάξω ὑμᾶς εἰς τὴν Γαλιλαίαν, but *after I have been raised,* I will go before you into Galilee (Mark 14:28)
- καὶ διερχόμενος εὐηγγελίζετο τὰς πόλεις πάσας ἕως τοῦ ἐλθεῖν αὐτὸν εἰς Καισάρειαν, and while passing through, he evangelized all the cities *until he came* to Caesarea (Acts 8:40)

6. **Infinitive of Purpose**. The infinitive of purpose often stands alone, but it may follow τοῦ, εἰς τό, πρὸς τό, ὥστε, or ὡς.

- Ἄνθρωποι δύο ἀνέβησαν εἰς τὸ ἱερὸν προσεύξασθαι, two men went up to the temple *to pray* (Luke 18:10)
- ἤλθομεν προσκυνῆσαι αὐτῷ, we have come *to worship* him (Matt. 2:2)

7. **Infinitive of Result**. The infinitive of result may stand alone, or it may follow τοῦ, εἰς τό, πρὸς τό, or ὥστε. The context must decide whether the author intended the infinitive to indicate purpose or result.

- ἡ πίστις ὑμῶν ἐξελήλυθεν, ὥστε μὴ χρείαν ἔχειν ἡμᾶς λαλεῖν τι, your faith has gone out, so that *we do not have* a need to say anything (1 Thess. 1:8)
- σκοτισθήτωσαν οἱ ὀφθαλμοὶ αὐτῶν τοῦ μὴ βλέπειν, let their eyes be darkened in order that *they should not see* [or,] with the result that *they do not see* (Rom. 11:10)

Note: The interpretation of εἰς τό with the infinitive is often important theologically. For example, was the revelation of God in nature (Rom. 1:20) designed *to make people inexcusable* when they sinned (*infinitive of purpose*), or did it reveal God clearly enough *that people were inexcusable* when they sinned (*infinitive of result*)? By itself, Greek grammar cannot resolve the question.

8. **Causal Infinitive**. The infinitive may be used to answer the question "Why?" The causal infinitive typically follows διὰ τό and is translated as *because* plus an indicative verb.

- καὶ διὰ τὸ μὴ ἔχειν ῥίζαν ἐξηράνθη, and *because it had* no root, it dried up (Mark 4:6)
- οὐκ ἔχετε διὰ τὸ μὴ αἰτεῖσθαι ὑμᾶς, you do not have *because you do not ask* (James 4:2)

9. **Imperatival Infinitive**. On rare occasions, the infinitive may stand alone as the main verb and be used to express a command. There are only a few New Testament examples of this use, and these may also be considered complementary or indirect-discourse infinitives with implied verbs.

- χαίρειν μετὰ χαιρόντων, κλαίειν μετὰ κλαιόντων, *rejoice* with those who rejoice; *weep* with those who weep (Rom. 12:15)
- πρεσβύτας νηφαλίους εἶναι, older men *are to be* sober minded (Titus 2:2)

Observing the Aspect of the Infinitive

As we have seen, *kind* of action is more significant than *time* of action in the Greek verb system. Thus it is always important to observe how the author wishes to describe the kind of action in the infinitive. Generally speaking, the aorist tense is the default tense, considering the action as undefined as far as progress, state, or completion (aoristic aspect). The present tense is used when progressive, repeated, or habitual action is described (imperfective aspect). The perfect tense indicates a state based on previous action (perfective aspect). Note the following examples:

- *Aorist* tense infinitive: μετὰ δὲ τὸ σιγῆσαι αὐτοὺς ἀπεκρίθη Ἰάκωβος, but *after they had become silent,* James answered [the *fact* of their silence is emphasized] (Acts 15:13)
- *Present* tense infinitive: διαπονούμενοι διὰ τὸ διδάσκειν αὐτοὺς τὸν λαόν, being annoyed *because they were teaching* the people [that is, they *kept on teaching* and refused to stop] (Acts 4:2)
- *Perfect* tense infinitive: πίστει νοοῦμεν κατηρτίσθαι τοὺς αἰῶνας ῥήματι θεοῦ, by faith we understand *the worlds to have been created* by the word of God [the focus is on the result of God's creative act: he not only created the universe but *maintains* it] (Heb. 11:3)

Conclusion

This chapter does not by any means exhaust the list of all the uses of the infinitive, but it does include the most important ones. At the table of the Greek parts of speech, there will always be a place of honor for the infinitive.

For Practice

Put into English the following sentences.

1. ὁ ἀπόστολος ἦλθεν ἰδεῖν τὸν λαὸν καὶ λαλῆσαι τὸν λόγον.
2. ἐγὼ μὲν χρείαν ἔχω βαπτισθῆναι ὑπὸ σοῦ, σὺ δὲ αἰτεῖς βαπτισθῆναι ὑπ᾿ ἐμοῦ;
3. ἐν τῇ βασιλείᾳ δεῖ ὑμᾶς γενέσθαι τέκνα πνευματικά.
4. οὐχ ἱκανός εἰμι διδάσκειν τὸν μαθητὴν ὃν ἔπεμψας.
5. μέλλομεν ποιεῖν μαθητὰς πάντων τῶν ἐθνῶν.
6. αὕτη ἐστὶν ἡ ὥρα τῆς μετανοίας. καιρὸς οὖν μετανοῆσαι.
7. ὁ Ἰησοῦς εἰσῆλθεν εἰς τὸν κόσμον πρὸς τὸ σῶσαι ἁμαρτωλούς.
8. διὰ τὸ θεραπεῦσαι τὸν Ἰησοῦν τοὺς ὀφθαλμοὺς αὐτῶν, οἱ τυφλοὶ ἐπίστευσαν ἐν αὐτῷ.
9. τὸ μὴ γινώσκειν τὴν ἀλήθειαν πονηρόν ἐστιν.
10. πρὸ τοῦ ἄρξασθαι τὸν ἀπόστολον κηρύσσειν τὸ εὐαγγέλιον, ὁ Ἰησοῦς ἤδη ἀνέβη πρὸς τὸν οὐρανόν.

11. διὰ τὸ ἐλθεῖν τὸν Ἰησοῦν εἰς τὸν οἶκον, οἱ μαθηταὶ αὐτοῦ εκήρυσσον.
12. μετὰ τὸ κηρῦξαι τὸν δοῦλον, ἄξομεν τοὺς ὄχλους πρὸς τὸν Ἰησοῦν.
13. τὸ φιλῆσαι καλόν ἐστιν.
14. ἦλθεν ὁ Ἰησοῦς πρὸς τὸ ἰδεῖν τοὺς μαθητάς.
15. ἀπήγαγον αὐτὸν εἰς τὸ σταυρῶσαι.
16. ἐνδύσασθε τὴν πανοπλίαν τοῦ θεοῦ πρὸς τὸ δυνάσθαι ὑμᾶς στῆναι.
17. οἶδεν ὁ πατὴρ ὑμῶν ὧν χρείαν ἔχετε πρὸ τοῦ ὑμᾶς αἰτῆσαι αὐτόν.
18. κατάβηθι πρὶν ἀποθανεῖν τὸ παιδίον μου.
19. οὐ δύνασθε θεῷ δουλεύειν καὶ μαμωνᾷ.
20. διδάσκειν δὲ γυναικὶ οὐκ ἐπιτρέπω οὐδὲ αὐθεντεῖν ἀνδρός, ἀλλ᾽ εἶναι ἐν ἡσυχίᾳ.
21. ὑμῖν ἐχαρίσθη τὸ ὑπὲρ Χριστοῦ, οὐ μόνον τὸ εἰς αὐτὸν πιστεύειν ἀλλὰ καὶ τὸ ὑπὲρ αὐτοῦ πάσχειν.
22. ἐλευθέρα ἐστὶν ᾧ θέλει γαμηθῆναι.
23. ἔστω πᾶς ἄνθρωπος ταχὺς εἰς τὸ ἀκοῦσαι, βραδὺς εἰς τὸ λαλῆσαι.
24. ἤμελλεν γὰρ ἀποθνήσκειν.
25. οὐκ ἔξεστίν σοι ἆραι τὸν κράββατόν σου.
26. ὑμεῖς δοκεῖτε ἐν αὐταῖς ζωὴν αἰώνιον ἔχειν.
27. ποιήσατε τοὺς ἀνθρώπους ἀναπεσεῖν.
28. ἤκουσαν τοῦτο αὐτὸν πεποιηκέναι τὸ σημεῖον.
29. δεῖ αὐτὸν ἐκ νεκρῶν ἀναστῆσαι.
30. ἀπὸ τότε ἤρξατο ὁ Ἰησοῦς δεικνύειν τοῖς μαθηταῖς αὐτοῦ ὅτι δεῖ αὐτὸν εἰς Ἰεροσόλυμα ἀπελθεῖν καὶ πολλὰ παθεῖν ἀπὸ τῶν πρεσβυτέρων καὶ ἀρχιερέων καὶ γραμματέων καὶ ἀποκτανθῆναι καὶ τῇ τρίτῃ ἡμέρᾳ ἐγερθῆναι.

Key Terms

causal infinitive
complementary infinitive
epexegetical infinitive
imperatival infinitive
infinitive of indirect discourse

infinitive of purpose
infinitive of result
infinitive of time
substantival infinitive

For Further Reading

Robertson 1050–95
Dana and Mantey 208–20
BDF 196–212
Zerwick 132–36
Wallace 587–611

11

Going, Going, Gone

The Participle

We have already learned something about participles in chapter 1. It was noted there that the participle is a verbal adjective, sharing the characteristics of both verbs and adjectives. As a verb, the participle has a subject and, if it is the participle of a verb in the active voice, it may have an object. As an adjective, it agrees with the noun that it qualifies in gender, number, and case.

This latter statement does not, of course, apply to English participles. When I was a schoolboy, a lot of useful fun was made of the "dangling" participle, and one I remember still amuses me today: "Did you see the grandfather clock coming upstairs?" In an inflected language like Greek this would be harmless enough. *Coming* would be nominative singular, and no ridiculous interpretation would occur to anyone. But in English we cannot assume that the juxtaposed *clock* and *coming* will be disassociated by a sudden onset of common sense.

In Greek, syntactical relationships are clearer, since they are grammatically fixed by inflections. To review:

- The active participles are declined with third-declension endings in the masculine and neuter, and first-declension endings in the feminine.
- The present middle and passive participle is declined like an adjective of the second declension.

- The aorist passive participles are declined with third-declension endings in the masculine and neuter and first-declension endings in the feminine.

For participle declensions, see your beginning grammar. Participles are generally negated by μή.

Uses of the Participle

As I have said before, participles are used more frequently in Greek than in English (there are 6,674 participles in the New Testament). Happily, there are only two main uses of the participle, and these are mastered easily enough. Participles may be used either adjectivally or adverbially.

1. The **adjectival participle** is generally preceded by an article with which it agrees. This so-called *arthrous participle* is occasionally used in English in expressions like *the living* and *the missing*. In the New Testament it is very common. The adjectival participle should normally be translated by a clause introduced by a relative pronoun but may sometimes be translated by a noun:

- οἱ πιστεύοντες, those who believe *or* the believers
- ὁ σπείρων, the one who sows *or* the sower
- οἱ πεινῶντες καὶ διψῶντες τὴν δικαιοσύνην, those who hunger and thirst after righteousness (Matt. 5:6)
- οὗτός ἐστιν ὁ παρὰ τὴν ὁδὸν σπαρείς, this is the one that was sown by the road (Matt. 13:19)

Notice in the final example above that in Greek any number of words may be inserted between the article and the participle.

Adjectival participles may also modify nouns and pronouns. Both the participle and the noun may have the article:

- καὶ ὁ διάβολος ὁ πλανῶν αὐτοὺς ἐβλήθη εἰς τὴν λίμνην τοῦ πυρός, and the devil *who deceived* them was thrown into the lake of fire (Rev. 20:10)
- καθὼς ἀπέστειλέν με ὁ ζῶν πατήρ, even as the *living* Father sent me (John 6:57)

2. The **adverbial participle** modifies some other verb in the sentence. Such participles are best translated by an English adverbial clause. The context determines what kind of adverbial clause the participle in ques-

tion is equivalent to. In the New Testament, an adverbial participle is often either **temporal** (indicating *when* an action takes place) or **causal** (indicating *why* an action takes place):

- καὶ ἐξελθὼν εἶδεν πολὺν ὄχλον, and *when he came out,* he saw a large crowd (Matt. 14:14)
- καὶ πάντες ἐφοβοῦντο αὐτόν, μὴ πιστεύοντες ὅτι ἐστὶν μαθητής, and all were afraid of him, *because they did not believe* that he was a disciple (Acts 9:26)

However, the adverbial participle can also denote attendant circumstances, in which case it is best translated into English by a finite verb accompanied by *and:*

- ἀποκριθεὶς εἶπεν, *he answered* and said
- εὐθὺς κράξας ὁ πατὴρ τοῦ παιδίου ἔλεγεν, and immediately the father of the boy *cried out* and said (Mark 9:24)

In other instances, the Greek participle is best translated by a simple English participle:

- ἐν δὲ ταῖς ἡμέραις ἐκείναις παραγίνεται Ἰωάννης ὁ βαπτιστὴς κηρύσσων ἐν τῇ ἐρήμῳ τῆς Ἰουδαίας καὶ λέγων, Μετανοεῖτε, in those days John the Baptist came into the wilderness of Judea *preaching* and *saying,* "Repent" (Matt. 3:1–2)

Other uses of the adverbial participle are much less frequent in the New Testament. For the sake of completeness I list them here:

- The **telic/final participle** indicates purpose (usually with the future participle). It is best translated by the English infinitive: ἴδωμεν εἰ ἔρχεται Ἠλίας σώσων αὐτόν, let us see if Elijah comes *to save* him (Matt. 27:49).
- The **conditional participle** is used in the *if* clause of a conditional statement: ἐξ ὧν διατηροῦντες ἑαυτοὺς εὖ πράξετε, from which, *if you keep* yourselves, you will do well (Acts 15:29).
- The **concessive participle** denotes a sense of—what else?—concession: εἰ γὰρ ἐχθροὶ ὄντες κατηλλάγημεν τῷ θεῷ, for if, *though we were* enemies, we were reconciled to God (Rom. 5:10).
- The **instrumental participle** indicates the means by which the action of the main verb is accomplished: ἐργασίαν πολλὴν παρεῖχεν . . . μαντευομένη, she brought much gain *by predicting the future* (Acts 16:16).

- The **complementary participle** is used to complete the idea of the action expressed in the main verb: οὐ παύομαι εὐχαριστῶν ὑπὲρ ὑμῶν, I do not cease *giving thanks* for you (Eph. 1:16).
- The **imperatival participle** is used to express a command: τῇ ἐλπίδι χαίροντες, τῇ θλίψει ὑπομένοντες, τῇ προσευχῇ προσκαρτεροῦντες, *rejoice* in hope, *be steadfast* in tribulation, *be devoted* to prayer (Rom. 12:12).
- The **periphrastic participle**, as we saw in chapter 8, uses a linking verb (usually a form of εἰμί) and the present- or perfect-tense participle to emphasize the aspect of the participle: χάριτί ἐστε σεσῳσμένοι, by grace *you have been saved* (Eph. 2:5).
- The **participle of attendant circumstance** (alluded to above) is used both to introduce a new action and to focus attention on the main verb. In this construction the tense of the participle is usually aorist, as is the tense of the main verb, and the participle precedes the verb: πορευθέντες δὲ μάθετε τί ἐστιν, now *go* and learn what this means (Matt. 9:13).
- The **participle absolute** involves a participle and noun or pronoun in the genitive case. The clause containing the participle is "loosed" from the rest of the sentence, and the construction is called *absolute* (from the Latin *absolutus*, "loosed"): καὶ ἐκβληθέντος τοῦ δαιμονίου ἐλάλησεν ὁ κωφός, and *when the demon had been thrown out*, the mute man spoke (Matt. 9:33). This construction is also called the **genitive absolute** (see chapter 3).

Of course, the participle itself contains none of the ideas presented above. It is only by observing the context that the significance of the participle can be determined.

The Meaning of Tense in the Participle

Though the tense of the participle never conveys an independent expression of time, it usually involves a temporal significance derived from the context. This is especially true of adverbial participles. Generally speaking, the present participle denotes action taking place *at the same time* as the action of the main verb (contemporaneous action), and the aorist participle denotes action that took place *before* the action of the main verb (antecedent action). (The future participle denotes time *subsequent* to that of the main verb; it is very rare in the New Testament.)

- Present participle denoting contemporaneous action: ὤφθη αὐτοῖς μαχομένοις, he appeared to them *while they were fighting* (Acts 7:26)

- Aorist participle denoting antecedent action: καὶ νηστεύσας ἡμέρας τεσσαράκοντα καὶ νύκτας τεσσαράκοντα ὕστερον ἐπείνασεν, and *after he had fasted* for forty days and forty nights, he afterwards became hungry (Matt. 4:2)

It is important to remember that these temporal relations are determined solely by the context and that there are many exceptions.

Conclusion

The number of words that fall into the category of participle is substantial. All of this elbow room is good news—if you have a firm handle on the subject. Meanwhile, the ruling consideration in interpreting participles is that they express something that is dependent on the main verb, as the sentences below amply illustrate.

For Practice

Put into English the following sentences.

1. ὑμεῖς οὖν ἀκούσατε τὴν παραβολὴν τοῦ σπείραντος.
2. καὶ ἦλθεν κηρύσσων εἰς τὰς συναγωγὰς αὐτῶν καὶ δαιμόνια ἐκβάλλων.
3. ἰδοὺ θεωρῶ τοὺς οὐρανοὺς διηνοιγμένους.
4. ζῶν ὁ λόγος τοῦ θεοῦ.
5. ἦσαν οἱ φαγόντες τοὺς ἄρτους πεντακισχίλιοι ἄνδρες.
6. τοῦτο δέ ἐστιν τὸ θέλημα τοῦ πέμψαντός με.
7. πᾶς ὁ ὄχλος ἰδόντες αὐτὸν ἐξεθαμβήθησαν.
8. ἀπῆλθεν λυπούμενος.
9. κοπιῶμεν ἐργαζόμενοι ταῖς ἰδίαις χερσίν.
10. ἑαυτὸν ἐκένωσεν μορφὴν δούλου λαβών.
11. θερίσομεν μὴ ἐκλυόμενοι.
12. γνόντες τὸν θεὸν οὐχ ὡς θεὸν ἐδόξασαν.
13. τοῦτο δὲ ἔλεγεν σημαίνων ποίῳ θανάτῳ ἤμελλεν ἀποθνήσκειν.
14. ἀπελθὼν δεῖξον σεαυτὸν τῷ ἱερεῖ.
15. ἰδὼν δὲ ὅτι ἀρεστόν ἐστιν τοῖς Ἰουδαίοις προσέθετο συλλαβεῖν καὶ Πέτρον.
16. τότε ὁ Παῦλος ἐκτείνας τὴν χεῖρα ἀπελογεῖτο.
17. ἀκούων δὲ ὁ Ἀνανίας τοὺς λόγους τούτους πεσὼν ἐξέψυξεν, καὶ ἐγένετο φόβος μέγας ἐπὶ πάντας τοὺς ἀκούοντας.
18. καίπερ ὢν υἱός, ἔμαθεν ἀφ᾽ ὧν ἔπαθεν τὴν ὑπακοήν.

19. ἦλθεν γὰρ Ἰωάννης μήτε ἐσθίων μήτε πίνων, καὶ λέγουσιν, Δαιμόνιον ἔχει.
20. οὐ πᾶς ὁ λέγων μοι, κύριε, κύριε, ἀγαθός ἐστιν, ἀλλ᾽ ὁ ποιῶν τὸ θέλημα τοῦ πατρός μου ἐν τοῖς οὐρανοῖς.
21. ἦν γὰρ διδάσκων αὐτοὺς ὡς ἐξουσίαν ἔχων, καὶ οὐχ ὡς οἱ γραμματεῖς αὐτῶν.
22. ἔτι δὲ λαλοῦντος τοῦ Πέτρου τὰ ῥήματα ταῦτα, ἔπεσεν τὸ πνεῦμα τὸ ἅγιον ἐπὶ πάντας τοὺς ἀκούσαντας τὸν λόγον.
23. ἰδὼν δὲ τοὺς ὄχλους ἀνέβη εἰς τὸ ὄρος. καὶ καθίσαντος αὐτοῦ προσῆλθον αὐτῷ οἱ μαθηταὶ αὐτοῦ. καὶ ἀνοίξας τὸ στόμα αὐτοῦ ἐδίδασκεν αὐτοὺς λέγων, Μακάριοι οἱ ὄντες πτωχοὶ τῷ πνεύματί εἰσιν, ὅτι αὐτῶν ἐστιν ἡ βασιλεία τῶν οὐρανῶν.

Key Terms

adjectival participle
adverbial participle
causal participle
complementary participle
concessive participle
conditional participle
final participle
genitive absolute

imperatival participle
instrumental participle
participle absolute
participle of attendant
  circumstance
periphrastic participle
telic participle
temporal participle

For Further Reading

Robertson 1095–1141
Dana and Mantey 220–33
BDF 212–20
Zerwick 125–31
Wallace 612–55

12

It's a Small Word after All

Adverbs, Conjunctions, and Particles

N ever start a sentence with *and.*"
Nobody seems to know where this widely disseminated kernel of advice on "good writing" first began to grow. The best explanation is that it took root when teachers tried to dissuade grade-schoolers from stringing together every sentence they wrote with one *and* after another.

Undoubtedly this guideline is worth remembering—but self-defeating if you follow it to the letter. Starting an occasional sentence with *and* is an effective way to smooth out the transition from one sentence to the next. After all, if there were anything unhealthy about the practice, the Bible would be forbidden reading in most grammar classes.

This chapter deals with adverbs, conjunctions, and particles—those "small" words of language. Often neglected in the study of grammar, they are important elements in a sentence.

Adverbs

The adverb is one of the eight basic parts of speech. **Adverbs** typically add specific information about time, manner, or place to the meaning of verbs in whole clauses. Thus there are adverbs of time, adverbs of manner, and adverbs of place. (These three categories don't actually cover everything that can be called an adverb).

Today, tomorrow, yesterday, then, now, soon, recently, and *always* are **adverbs of time**: they add information about the time when something happens.

Slowly, quickly, fast, early, badly, and *well* are **adverbs of manner**: they add information about the manner in which something is done.

Here, there, somewhere, anywhere, and *everywhere* are **adverbs of place**: they add information about the place where something happens.

In English, many adverbs of manner are formed by adding the suffix *-ly* to an adjective: *slow* (adjective), *slowly* (adverb). Adverbs may be placed at the beginning, middle, or end of a clause with a slight difference of emphasis. Adverbs are always optional elements of clauses: if you omit an adverb, you get less information, but the clause still makes sense without it.

Some languages don't have adverbs as a separate part of speech. German, for example, mainly uses its adjectives for adverbs, allowing them to modify verbs as well as nouns. Thus German uses one word *(schnell)* for both *quick* and *quickly,* and one word *(gut)* for both *good* and *well.* Nonstandard English sometimes does the same thing: "She did it *good*" (a sentence that uses no adverbs) is another way of saying "She did it *well.*"

In Greek, all adverbs originally had clear-cut case forms like nouns. So it need not surprise us to find a noun, pronoun, or participle used adverbially. The most common adverbial suffix in the New Testament is -ως, a survival of an old genitive case ending. Thus we have ὁμολογουμένως, *confessedly* (1 Tim. 3:16); κακῶς, *badly* (Matt. 14:35); σπουδαιοτέρως, *more zealously* (Phil. 2:28); ἐσχάτως, *extremely* (Mark 5:23); and about a hundred other adverbs ending in -ως. Other adverbial case suffixes include:

- Nominative: ἅπαξ, *once* (2 Cor. 11:25)
- Genitive: ὅπου, *where* (Matt. 6:19)
- Dative: κύκλῳ, *in a circle* (Mark 3:34)
- Accusative: δωρεάν, *freely* (Matt. 10:8)

Other than possessing these original case suffixes, adverbs are never inflected. Their spelling always remains the same, with the exception of the movable ς, as with οὕτω(ς), *thus.*

The following New Testament adverbs occur frequently and should be memorized:

- **Adverbs of time**: τότε *(then),* νῦν *(now),* ἤδη *(already),* σήμερον *(today),* πάλιν *(again)*
- **Adverbs of manner**: οὕτως *(thus, in this manner),* καλῶς *(rightly, well),* ὁμοίως *(likewise, similarly),* ἀληθῶς *(truly),* ταχέως *(quickly)*

- **Adverbs of place**: ἐκεῖ *(there)*, ἔξω *(outside)*, ὧδε *(here)*, ἐκεῖθεν *(from there)*, ποῦ *(somewhere)*
- **Interrogative adverbs**: πῶς *(how?)*, ποῦ *(where?)*, πόθεν *(from where?)*, πότε *(when?)*
- **Numerical adverbs**: ἅπαξ *(once)*, δίς *(two times)*, τρίς *(three times)*, ἑπτάκις *(seven times)*
- **Adverbs of degree**: λίαν *(very)*, μάλιστα *(especially)*, μᾶλλον *(rather, more)*, σφόδρα *(extremely)*

In interpreting these adverbs, four rules should be remembered.

1. An adverb usually modifies the verb *closest* to it.
2. Adverbs of time and manner usually *precede* the word they modify: ἐβουλήθη λάθρα ἀπολῦσαι αὐτήν, he desired to divorce her *secretly* [not, "he *secretly* desired to divorce her"] (Matt. 1:19).
3. Adverbs of place usually *follow* the word modified: καὶ προβὰς ἐκεῖθεν εἶδεν ἄλλους δύο ἀδελφούς, and when he went on *from there*, he saw two other brothers [not, "and when he went on, *from there* he saw two other brothers"] (Matt. 4:21).
4. Adverbs can modify verbs, adjectives, and other adverbs, though sometimes they function as nouns:

    - ἐγὼ σήμερον γεγέννηκά σε, *today* I have begotten you [modifying a verb] (Heb. 1:5)
    - ὁμολογουμένως μέγα ἐστὶν τὸ τῆς εὐσεβείας μυστήριον, *confessedly* great is the secret of godliness [modifying an adjective] (1 Tim. 3:16)
    - ἔτι ἅπαξ ἐγὼ σείσω οὐ μόνον τὴν γῆν ἀλλὰ καὶ τὸν οὐρανόν, *once* more I will shake not only the earth but the heaven also [modifying an adverb] (Heb. 12:26)
    - οὐχ ὁ ποιήσης τὸ ἔξωθεν καὶ τὸ ἔσωθεν ἐποίησεν, did not the one who made *the outside* make *the inside* also? [functioning as a noun] (Luke 11:40)

Conjunctions

The **conjunction** is that part of speech that connects words, phrases, clauses, or sentences, or that shows relationships between sentences. Conjunctions are essential to the balance, rhythm, and structure of sentences; the wrong choice can shift the weight, alter the tempo, splatter the punctuation, fragment the meaning, joggle the transition, and sink the sentence or give it a seasick lurch. In the New Testament, conjunctions are important gap-fillers, the cartilage at the joints of speech.

There are two main classes of conjunctions: coordinating and subordinating. A **coordinating conjunction** is one that joins two coordinate elements, that is, elements of equal order or rank—two nouns, two verbs, two phrases, or two clauses, neither of which is dependent on the other, as in "You *and* I like fruit." A **subordinating conjunction** is one that joins a subordinate element to the principal element of the sentence: "*When* John spoke, everybody listened."

Subordinating conjunctions generally denote the following relations:

- Time: *when, since, until, as long as, as soon as,* etc.
- Reason, cause, or concession: *as, because, for, since, although,* etc.
- Contingency or supposition: *if, though, unless, provided,* etc.
- Purpose, result, or content: *in order that, so that, that,* etc.
- Comparison: *than, otherwise, rather,* etc.

You will recall from chapter 2 that compound sentences are comprised of independent clauses. The independent clauses of compound sentences are joined by coordinating conjunctions. The subordinate clauses of complex sentences are joined to main clauses by subordinating conjunctions. Subordinating conjunctions are more difficult because there are more of them and because the function of connecting subordinate clauses is more subtle than coupling equal elements.

English conjunctions are generally positioned at the beginning of the sentence or the clause that they are joining to the preceding sentence or clause. In Greek, however, several conjunctions are **postpositive**, that is, they cannot stand first in their sentence or clause. Postpositive conjunctions include ἄρα, γάρ, δέ, οὖν, and τε.

Sometimes a conjunction is not used where an English reader would expect it. This is called **asyndeton**, meaning "not bound together" (ἀσύνδετον). When asyndeton occurs between words or phrases, it suggests excitement or urgency. When asyndeton occurs between paragraphs, it usually indicates the introduction of a new subject. In a long series of coordinate nouns, adjectives, or verbs, conjunctions are more often omitted than inserted (see Luke 6:27–28; John 5:3, 8; Rom. 1:29–31; 1 Thess. 5:15–22).

Coordinating Conjunctions

Let's now take a closer look at conjunctions that unite elements of equal rank. (These are also called **paratactic conjunctions**.) There are five main classes of coordinating conjunctions in the New Testament.

1. **Copulative conjunctions** simply "couple together" without stating the relationship between the elements united.

- καί, the most frequently used conjunction in the New Testament, is usually copulative (*and*). Sometimes it is used adverbially (*also, even*): ἀληθῶς καὶ σὺ ἐξ αὐτῶν εἶ, truly you *also* are [one] of them (Matt. 26:73).
- τε, meaning *and*, indicates a slightly closer connection than καί. It is a common conjunction in Acts: χάρις τε μεγάλη ἦν ἐπὶ πάντας αὐτούς, *and* much grace was upon them all (Acts 4:33).
- δέ may have a copulative use *(and, now)*, though it frequently has an adversative sense *(but)*. The copulative force is clearly seen in the genealogy of Matthew 1:2–16.
- ἀλλά most often means *but* (see below), though this is not its only meaning. Like δέ, the thing introduced by ἀλλά is new but not necessarily in contrast to something else.

2. **Adversative conjunctions** imply contrast or antithesis. The context will indicate how strong the contrast is.

- ἀλλά usually implies a strong contrast: θεὸς δὲ οὐκ ἔστιν νεκρῶν ἀλλὰ ζώντων, now he is not the God of the dead *but* of the living (Luke 20:38). Ἀλλά has also been called an **eliminative adversative** since it is used where one of two contrasted members is negated, the true being substituted for the false.
- δέ is frequently adversative (though not as strong as ἀλλά): ἐγὼ ἐβάπτισα ὑμᾶς ὕδατι, αὐτὸς δὲ βαπτίσει ὑμᾶς πνεύματι ἁγίῳ, I baptized you with water, *but* he himself will baptize you with the Holy Spirit (Mark 1:8). In contrast to ἀλλά, δέ is a **balancing adversative**, used when two truths of divergent tendency are presented.

3. **Disjunctive conjunctions** indicate a contrast or an alternative between words or clauses.

- ἤ *(or)* is mutually exclusive: μενέτω ἄγαμος ἢ τῷ ἀνδρὶ καταλλαγήτω, let her remain unmarried *or* be reconciled to her husband (1 Cor. 7:11).
- εἴτε . . . εἴτε means *whether . . . or*: ἵνα εἴτε γρηγορῶμεν εἴτε καθεύδωμεν ἅμα σὺν αὐτῷ ζήσωμεν, in order that *whether* we are awake *or* asleep, we will live together with him (1 Thess. 5:10).

4. **Inferential conjunctions** are used to draw a conclusion from a truth just stated or to indicate a result from what has preceded.

- ἄρα *(therefore, then)* is nearly always inferential in the New Testament: εἰ γὰρ διὰ νόμου δικαιοσύνη, ἄρα Χριστὸς δωρεὰν ἀπέθανεν, for if righteousness [comes] through the Law, *then* Christ died for no purpose (Gal. 2:21).
- διό and διόπερ both mean *for this reason, therefore:* διὸ οὐδὲ ἐμαυτὸν ἠξίωσα πρὸς σὲ ἐλθεῖν, *therefore*, neither did I count myself worthy to come to you (Luke 7:7).
- οὖν is the most common inferential conjunction in the New Testament, occurring some four hundred times. It is usually translated as *therefore* or *then:* μετανοήσατε οὖν καὶ ἐπιστρέψατε, repent, *therefore*, and turn (Acts 3:19). But a warning is necessary here. Οὖν sometimes has merely a continuative force, especially in the Gospel of John, where it loosely strings clauses and sentences together (for numerous examples, see John 11).

5. Finally, the main **causal conjunction** in the New Testament is γάρ (*for*): τέξεται δὲ υἱόν, καὶ καλέσεις τὸ ὄνομα αὐτοῦ Ἰησοῦν· αὐτὸς γὰρ σώσει τὸν λαὸν αὐτοῦ ἀπὸ τῶν ἁμαρτιῶν αὐτῶν, "and she will give birth to a son, and you are to call his name Jesus; *for* he himself will save his people from their sins" (Matt. 1:21).

Subordinating Conjunctions

Subordinating conjunctions (also called **hypotactic conjunctions**) introduce grammatically dependent clauses that express such ideas as purpose, result, cause, condition, comparison, concession, and time. These functions are indicated by the following conjunctions:

- ἵνα with the subjunctive generally expresses purpose: τεκνία μου, ταῦτα γράφω ὑμῖν ἵνα μὴ ἁμάρτητε, my little children, I am writing these things to you *in order that* you may not sin (1 John 2:1). Do not think, however, that ἵνα always means *in order that*. It often introduces a substantive clause: καὶ αὕτη ἐστὶν ἡ ἀγάπη, ἵνα περιπατῶμεν κατὰ τὰς ἐντολὰς αὐτοῦ, and this is love, *that* we should walk according to his commands (2 John 6).
- ὅπως with the subjunctive may introduce purpose: ἀπαγγείλατέ μοι, ὅπως κἀγὼ ἐλθὼν προσκυνήσω αὐτῷ, report to me, *in order that* I too may go and worship him (Matt. 2:8). Note that ἵνα and ὅπως are often used synonymously. Compare Matthew 1:22 (ἵνα πληρωθῇ τὸ ῥηθέν) and Matthew 2:23 (ὅπως πληρωθῇ τὸ ῥηθέν): *in order that* what had been spoken might be fulfilled.

- ὥστε normally indicates result, effect, or consequence: συνήχθη-σαν πολλοὶ ὥστε μηκέτι χωρεῖν, many were assembled there, *so that* there was no more room (Mark 2:2).
- ὅτι primarily indicates cause or reason: ὅτι οὐκ εἰμὶ χείρ, οὐκ εἰμὶ ἐκ τοῦ σώματος, *because* I am not a hand, I do not belong to the body (1 Cor. 12:15). ὅτι may also introduce content clauses: ἐν τούτῳ ἐστὶν ἡ ἀγάπη, οὐχ ὅτι ἠγαπήκαμεν τὸν θεόν, ἀλλ᾽ ὅτι αὐτὸς ἠγάπησεν ἡμᾶς, In this is love, not *that* we have loved God, but *that* he himself loved us (1 John 4:10).
- ἐπεί often has the meaning *since* or *because*: ἐπεὶ κατ᾽ οὐδένος εἶχεν μείζονος ὀμόσαι, ὤμοσεν καθ᾽ ἑαυτοῦ, *since* he could swear by no one greater, he swore by himself (Heb. 6:13).
- ὡς typically expresses a comparison between two words, phrases, or clauses: ἡμέρα κυρίου ὡς κλέπτης ἐν νυκτὶ οὕτως ἔρχεται, the day of the Lord will so come *like* a thief in the night (1 Thess. 5:2). Ὡς may also be used as a temporal conjunction and be translated *when, after, while,* or *as:* ὡς ἀτενίζοντες ἦσαν εἰς τὸν οὐρανὸν πορευομέ-νου αὐτοῦ, *while* they were watching him go into heaven (Acts 1:10).
- ὡσεί usually indicates comparison: ὡσεὶ περιβόλαιον ἑλίξεις αὐ-τούς, *like* a cloak you will roll them up (Heb. 1:12).
- εἰ expresses *if* in a conditional clause that uses the indicative mood: εἰ δὲ Χριστὸς οὐκ ἐγήγερται, ματαία ἡ πίστις ὑμῶν, but *if* Christ has not been raised, your faith [is] in vain (1 Cor. 15:17).
- ἐάν expresses *if* in a conditional clause that uses the subjunc-tive: ἐὰν γὰρ ἀγαπήσητε τοὺς ἀγαπῶντας ὑμᾶς, τίνα μισθὸν ἔχετε, for *if* you love those who love you, what reward do you have? (Matt. 5:46).
- εἰ καί, ἐὰν καί, καὶ ἐάν, and κἄν (a combination of καὶ ἐάν) may all be used to indicate concession: εἰ γὰρ καὶ τῇ σαρκὶ ἄπειμι, ἀλλὰ τῷ πνεύματι σὺν ὑμῖν εἰμι, for *although* I am absent in the flesh, yet I am with you in the spirit (Col. 2:5).
- ὅτε with the indicative is a temporal conjunction indicating a time frame within which something takes place: νῦν γὰρ ἐγγύτερον ἡμῶν ἡ σωτηρία ἢ ὅτε ἐπιστεύσαμεν, for now our salvation is nearer than *when* we believed (Rom. 13:11).
- ἕως with the subjunctive has the meaning *while* or *until:* καθίσατε ὧδε ἕως προσεύξωμαι, sit here *while* I pray (Mark 14:32).
- ὅταν with the subjunctive may be translated *whenever* or *when:* χαίρομεν γὰρ ὅταν ἡμεῖς ἀσθενῶμεν, we rejoice *whenever* we are weak (2 Cor. 13:9).

Particles

Particles are small words that don't easily fit into any clear-cut word class. It is thus something of a "cop-out category" for grammarians: if it's small and you don't know what to call it, call it a particle. Some grammarians use the term to include adverbs, prepositions, conjunctions, and interjections. I am using it in a more restricted sense to refer to negative and emphatic particles, including interjections. (Don't confuse *particle* with the similar-looking *participle*. The latter has a much more well-defined application.)

Negative Particles

There are two simple **negative particles** in Greek, οὐ (also written οὐκ and οὐχ) and μή. The particle οὐ is used for a clear-cut denial: οὐκ οἴδαμεν, "we do *not* know" (Matt. 21:27). It is the natural negative to use with the indicative mood. The emphatic form, οὐχί, is used for strong denial: οὐχί, ἀλλὰ κληθήσεται Ἰωάννης, "*No!* But he will be called John" (Luke 1:60). Οὐ has several compounds, including οὐδείς, οὐδέ, οὔτε, and οὐκέτι.

The particle μή is the negative used for hypothetical or hesitant denial. It is quite natural that μή should be used with the subjunctive, optative, and imperative moods. Μή is frequently used with the aorist subjunctive and the present imperative to express prohibition. With the aorist subjunctive it has an ingressive force ("don't *begin* to do") or a general meaning ("do *not* do"). With the present imperative it either means "*stop* what you are doing" or "make it your habit *not* to do." If the action is clearly in progress, the former meaning is in view: μὴ θησαυρίζετε, "*stop* laying up treasures" (Matt. 6:19). If the action has not begun, this would mean "make it your habit *not* to lay up treasures." Μή has a number of compounds, including μηδέ, μηδείς, and μηδέπω.

In standard English, only one negative element can normally stand in a clause. In many nonstandard English dialects, however, multiple negation is quite common: "I don't got no money." Greek has a double-negation construction that is very emphatic: οὐ μή. It may be translated *certainly not, never,* or *by no means:* οὐ μὴ εἰσέλθητε εἰς τὴν βασιλείαν τῶν οὐρανῶν, "you will *certainly not* enter the kingdom of heaven" (Matt. 5:20).

Emphatic Particles

Emphatic particles express fine shades of thought or emotion. They are inserted in the sentence to emphasize some word or the thought of the sentence as a whole. Emphatic particles may be compared to the marks of expression in a musical score (e.g., *con spirito*, play in a lively manner; *dolce*, play softly, sweetly), which suggest interpretation rather than dictate it. In this sense, a page from Paul's writings bears some resemblance to a page from Bach or Beethoven.

In contrast with Classical Greek, there are comparatively few emphatic particles in the New Testament—a fact that makes their use all the more significant. The following particles deserve special mention:

- ἀμήν is a transliteration of a Hebrew verbal adjective that means *to be firm*. It is commonly used to express assent to prayers: ὁ δὲ θεὸς τῆς εἰρήνης μετὰ πάντων ὑμῶν. ἀμήν, and the God of peace will be with you. *Amen* (Rom. 15:33). In the Gospels, it is frequently used by Jesus to introduce a solemn statement: ἀμὴν λέγω ὑμῖν, ἐὰν μὴ στραφῆτε καὶ γένησθε ὡς τὰ παιδία, οὐ μὴ εἰσέλθητε εἰς τὴν βασιλείαν τῶν οὐρανῶν, *truly* I tell you, unless you turn and become like little children, you will certainly not enter the kingdom of heaven (Matt. 18:3).
- ἄν implies uncertainty or vagueness and generally imparts the meaning *-ever*: ὅταν ("whenever"), ὃς ἄν ("whoever"), etc.
- γε emphasizes the word with which it is used and may be translated *at least, indeed, even,* or *in fact:* εἴ γε ἠκούσατε τὴν οἰκονομίαν τῆς χάριτος τοῦ θεοῦ, if, *in fact*, you heard of the administration of the grace of God (Eph. 3:2).
- ἴδε is the second person singular active imperative of εἶδον. It is a stereotyped particle in the New Testament and means *see* or *here is:* ἴδε ὁ τόπος ὅπου ἔθηκαν αὐτόν, *here is* the place where they laid him (Mark 16:6). Ἰδού (middle imperative) is used in the same way: ἰδοὺ ἡ μήτηρ μου, *here is* my mother (Matt. 12:49).
- μέν is an affirmative, adversative, or emphatic particle. When it is used with the article, the expression may be translated as a pronoun: οἱ μὲν ἔλεγον, *some* were saying (John 7:12). Other renderings include *in fact, rather, on the one hand, indeed*.
- ναί is a strong emphatic particle with the significance of *indeed* or *certainly:* ναὶ λέγω ὑμῖν, ἐκζητηθήσεται ἀπὸ τῆς γενεᾶς ταύτης, *indeed*, I tell you, it will be required of this generation (Luke 11:51).

Conclusion

Small words such as adverbs, conjunctions, and particles are important—despite their size. I hope I do not shock you when I say that

Χριστός is no more inspired than οὐ. Small words are still included in the *all* that is part of God-breathed Scripture (2 Tim. 3:16). In fact, you can't decide the meaning of a passage until you understand the flow of the author's thought, and this is impossible without understanding small words. If you want to do a thorough job of exegesis, you must take a look at the little guys and not only the big shots. If you devote considerable time to this practice now, I guarantee that it will pay you rich dividends later on.

For Practice

Put into English the following passage, noting especially the adverbs, conjunctions, and particles.

Ὅτε οὖν ἠρίστησαν λέγει τῷ Σίμωνι Πέτρῳ ὁ Ἰησοῦς· Σίμων Ἰωάννου, ἀγαπᾷς με πλέον τούτων; λέγει αὐτῷ· ναὶ κύριε, σὺ οἶδας ὅτι φιλῶ σε. λέγει αὐτῷ· βόσκε τὰ ἀρνία μου. λέγει αὐτῷ πάλιν δεύτερον· Σίμων Ἰωάννου, ἀγαπᾷς με; λέγει αὐτῷ· ναὶ κύριε, σὺ οἶδας ὅτι φιλῶ σε. λέγει αὐτῷ· ποίμαινε τὰ πρόβατά μου. λέγει αὐτῷ τὸ τρίτον· Σίμων Ἰωάννου, φιλεῖς με; ἐλυπήθη ὁ Πέτρος ὅτι εἶπεν αὐτῷ τὸ τρίτον· φιλεῖς με; καὶ λέγει αὐτῷ· κύριε, πάντα σὺ οἶδας, σὺ γινώσκεις ὅτι φιλῶ σε. λέγει αὐτῷ ὁ Ἰησοῦς· βόσκε τὰ πρόβατά μου. ἀμὴν ἀμὴν λέγω σοι, ὅτε ἦς νεώτερος, ἐζώννυες σεαυτὸν καὶ περιεπάτεις ὅπου ἤθελες· ὅταν δὲ γηράσῃς, ἐκτενεῖς τὰς χεῖράς σου, καὶ ἄλλος σε ζώσει καὶ οἴσει ὅπου οὐ θέλεις. τοῦτο δὲ εἶπεν σημαίνων ποίῳ θανάτῳ δοξάσει τὸν θεόν. καὶ τοῦτο εἰπὼν λέγει αὐτῷ· ἀκολούθει μοι.

Key Terms

adverb of degree
adverb of manner
adverb of place
adverb of time
adverb
adversative conjunction
asyndeton
balancing adversative
causal conjunction
conjunction
coordinating conjunction
copulative conjunction

disjunctive conjunction
eliminative adversative
emphatic particle
hypotactic conjunction
inferential conjunction
interrogative adverb
negative particle
numerical adverb
paratactic conjunction
particle
postpositive
subordinating conjunction

For Further Reading

Robertson 544–52; 1142–93
Dana and Mantey 234–67
BDF 220–39
Zerwick 137–60
Wallace 666–78

PART 4

From Alpha to Omega

Finishing Touches

13

A Cure for *Clause*trophobia

Greek Clauses

As we saw in chapter 2, there are two basic types of **clauses**: independent (main) and dependent (subordinate). An independent clause can stand alone as a sentence. A dependent clause cannot stand alone as a sentence; its dependence on the main clause is signaled by a subordinating conjunction, relative pronoun, or some other grammatical feature that indicates subordination. Every sentence contains an independent clause, and every independent clause contains a simple subject and a simple predicate, which can be expanded with single words, phrases, and dependent clauses.

The following are the most common types of clauses found in the New Testament.

Temporal Clauses

A **temporal clause** denotes the time of the action of the verb in the main clause on which it depends. Temporal clauses are frequently introduced by ὅτε, ὡς, or ὅταν, meaning *when* or *whenever*.

- ὅτε ἐτέλεσεν ὁ Ἰησοῦς τοὺς λόγους τούτους, μετῆρεν, *when* Jesus had finished these words, he left (Matt. 19:1)

141

- ὅταν στήκετε προσευχόμενοι, ἀφίετε, *whenever* you stand up to pray, forgive (Mark 11:25)

They may also be introduced by ἕως, ἄχρι οὗ, or ἐφ᾽ ὅσον, meaning *while*.

- ἠνάγκασεν τοὺς μαθητὰς . . . ἐμβῆναι . . . ἕως . . . ἀπολύει τὸν ὄχλον, he ordered the disciples to get into the boat *while* he dismissed the crowd (Mark 6:45)

Or they may be introduced by ἕως, ἄχρι, ἄχρι οὗ, μέχρι, or μέχρι οὗ, meaning *until*.

- ὁ ἀστὴρ . . . προῆγεν αὐτοὺς ἕως ἐστάθη ἐπάνω οὗ ἦν τὸ παιδίον, the star went ahead of them *until* it stood over the place where the child was (Matt. 2:9)

In addition, great numbers of temporal clauses are expressed in Greek by the use of participles, either in agreement with words in the sentence or in the genitive absolute. Likewise, temporal clauses can be expressed by prepositions with the arthrous infinitive (ἐν τῷ = *while*, πρὸ τοῦ = *before*, μετὰ τό = *after*, ἕως τοῦ = *until*).

Relative Clauses

Relative clauses are most frequently introduced by the relative pronoun ὅς. When a pronoun introduces a relative clause it functions as a part of speech within that clause (i.e., as subject, indirect object, object, etc.).

- ἐσαλεύθη ὁ τόπος ἐν ᾧ ἦσαν συνηγμένοι, the place *in which* they were gathered was shaken (Acts 4:31)
- κράτει ὃ ἔχεις, hold fast *that which* you have (Rev. 3:11)

Comparative Clauses

Comparative clauses are most frequently introduced by ὡς, ὡσεί, ὥσπερ, καθώς, and καθάπερ.

- ὀψόμεθα αὐτὸν καθώς ἐστιν, we will see him *as* he is (1 John 3:2)
- ὅτε ἤμην νήπιος, ἐλάλουν ὡς νήπιος, when I was a child, I used to speak *like* a child (1 Cor. 13:11)

Causal Clauses

Causal clauses are most frequently introduced by ὅτι, γάρ, διότι, καθότι, ἐπεί, ἐπειδή, ὅθεν, ἐφ᾽ ᾧ, ἐφ᾽ ὅσον, and οὗ χάριν. (The infinitive and participle may also be used in causal clauses.)

- οὐκ ἤφιεν λαλεῖν τὰ δαιμόνια, ὅτι ἤδεισαν αὐτόν, he would not let the demons speak, *because* they knew him (Mark 1:34)
- μάρτυς γάρ μού ἐστιν ὁ θεός, *for* God is my witness (Rom. 1:9)

Local Clauses

Local clauses are introduced by a relative adverb of place: ὅπου, οὗ, or ὅθεν.

- καὶ ἄλλο ἔπεσεν ἐπὶ τὸ πετρῶδες ὅπου οὐκ εἶχεν γῆν πολλήν, and the other [seed] fell on stony ground, *where* it didn't have much soil (Mark 4:5)
- ἀναπτύξας τὸ βιβλίον εὗρεν τὸν τόπον οὗ ἦν γεγραμμένον, when he opened the book, he found the place *where* it was written (Luke 4:17)

Purpose Clauses

Purpose may be expressed in several ways: most commonly by ἵνα and ὅπως, meaning *that, in order that;* by the simple infinitive; by the infinitive with τοῦ; by the arthrous infinitive with εἰς and πρός; and, rarely, by the relative pronoun with the future indicative or the subjunctive; and by the future and present participle.

- ἦλθεν . . . ἵνα μαρτυρήσῃ περὶ τοῦ φωτός, he came *in order that he might testify* about the light (John 1:7)
- μὴ νομίσητε ὅτι ἦλθον καταλῦσαι τὸν νόμον, do not think that I came *to destroy* the law (Matt. 5:17)
- μέλλει γὰρ Ἡρῴδης ζητεῖν τὸ παιδίον τοῦ ἀπολέσαι αὐτό, for Herod is about to look for the child *to destroy* it (Matt. 2:13)
- πᾶς ὁ βλέπων γυναῖκα πρὸς τὸ ἐπιθυμῆσαι αὐτὴν ἤδη ἐμοίχευσεν αὐτὴν ἐν τῇ καρδίᾳ αὐτοῦ, everyone who looks at a woman *for the purpose of desiring* her has already committed adultery with her in his heart (Matt. 5:28)

It should be noted that there are many passages where ἵνα with the subjunctive and τοῦ with the infinitive have lost all, or nearly all, of the idea of purpose and instead play the part of simple noun clauses. These instances should be carefully noted in exegesis (e.g., Acts 10:25: ἐγένετο τοῦ εἰσελθεῖν, "so it was that he entered").

Result Clauses

Result clauses express what issues from the action of the main verb. Most frequently, result is indicated by ὥστε and the infinitive; the simple infinitive or the infinitive with τοῦ is less commonly used.

- καὶ ἐθαμβήθησαν ἅπαντες ὥστε συζητεῖν πρὸς ἑαυτούς, and all of them were amazed, *so that they were debating* with each other (Mark 1:27)
- ἐλευθέρα ἐστὶν ἀπὸ τοῦ νόμου, τοῦ μὴ εἶναι αὐτὴν μοιχαλίδα, she is free from the law, *so that she is not* an adulteress (Rom. 7:3)

Content Clauses

Content clauses involve a subject, predicate nominative, direct object, or an appositional noun clause. Such clauses are commonly introduced by ἵνα, ὅτι, ὅπως, and ὡς.

- ζητεῖται ἐν τοῖς οἰκονόμοις, ἵνα πιστός τις εὑρεθῇ, it is sought in stewards *that* a person be found faithful (1 Cor. 4:2)
- κύριε, θεωρῶ ὅτι προφήτης εἶ σύ, sir, I see *that* you are a prophet (John 4:19)

Conditional Clauses

A conditional sentence has two parts: an "if" clause (the **protasis**), and a "then" clause (the **apodosis**): "If God is for us, then who can be against us?" Only the apodosis can stand alone as a sentence ("Then who can be against us?"). The protasis ("If God is for us"), on the other hand, is grammatically dependent on the apodosis. There are four general types of conditional sentences in the New Testament.

The **first-class condition** (also called the **simple condition**) assumes the reality of the protasis for the sake of argument. (Objectively speaking, the statement may or may not be true). In the protasis, the particle εἰ is used with the indicative mood, while in the apodosis any mood and any tense can occur. This is a frequent New Testament conditional clause, occurring some three hundred times.

- εἰ δὲ πνεύματι ἄγεσθε, οὐκ ἐστὲ ὑπὸ νόμον, but *if* you are being led by the Spirit, you are not under law (Gal. 5:18)

The **second-class condition** (also called the **contrary-to-fact condition**) assumes the unreality of the protasis for the sake of argument. The protasis contains εἰ with a secondary tense of the indicative (usually the aorist or the imperfect), and the apodosis has ἄν and a secondary tense of the indicative. There are about fifty occurrences of the second-class condition in the New Testament.

- εἰ . . . ἐπιστεύετε Μωϋσεῖ, ἐπιστεύετε ἄν ἐμοί, *if* you had believed Moses, you would have believed me (John 5:46)

Here the idea is: "If you had believed Moses (and you didn't!). . . ."

The **third-class condition** (also called the **more-probable future condition**) presents the condition as uncertain of fulfillment, though still likely. The protasis has ἐάν or ἐάνπερ followed by the subjunctive in any tense; the apodosis can have any mood and any tense. This class of condition occurs about three hundred times in the New Testament.

- καὶ τοῦτο ποιήσομεν, ἐάνπερ ἐπιτρέπῃ ὁ θεός, and this we will do, *if* God permits (Heb. 6:3)

Finally, the **fourth-class condition** (also called the **less-probable future condition**) indicates a possible condition in the future but one that is very remote. The protasis has εἰ with the optative mood; the optative is also used in the apodosis along with ἄν. There is no complete example of this class of condition in the New Testament, due in large part to the decrease in the use of the optative in Koine Greek.

- εἰ καὶ πάσχοιτε διὰ δικαιοσύνην, μακάριοι, even *if* you should suffer for righteousness, [you would be] blessed (1 Pet. 3:14)

Conclusion

At all times it is necessary to deduce from the context the exact meaning of each of these constructions. No set of rules applies. A clear understanding of the immediate context, coupled with a good dose of common sense, is better than all the rules that could be devised.

For Practice

Put into English the following passage.

Τὸν μὲν πρῶτον λόγον ἐποιησάμην περὶ πάντων, ὦ Θεόφιλε, ὧν ἤρξατο ὁ Ἰησοῦς ποιεῖν τε καὶ διδάσκειν, ἄχρι ἧς ἡμέρας ἐντειλάμενος τοῖς ἀποστόλοις διὰ πνεύματος ἁγίου οὓς ἐξελέξατο ἀνελήμφθη. οἷς καὶ παρέστησεν ἑαυτὸν ζῶντα μετὰ τὸ παθεῖν αὐτὸν ἐν πολλοῖς τεκμηρίοις, δι' ἡμερῶν τεσσεράκοντα ὀπτανόμενος αὐτοῖς καὶ λέγων τὰ περὶ τῆς βασιλείας τοῦ θεοῦ· καὶ συναλιζόμενος παρήγγειλεν αὐτοῖς ἀπὸ Ἰεροσολύμων μὴ χωρίζεσθαι ἀλλὰ περιμένειν τὴν ἐπαγγελίαν τοῦ πατρὸς ἣν ἠκούσατέ μου, ὅτι Ἰωάννης μὲν ἐβάπτισεν ὕδατι, ὑμεῖς δὲ ἐν πνεύματι βαπτισθήσεσθε ἁγίῳ οὐ μετὰ πολλὰς ταύτας ἡμέρας.

Key Terms

apodosis	local clause
causal clause	more-probable future condition
clause	protasis
comparative clause	purpose clause
conditional clause	relative clause
content clause	result clause
contrary-to-fact condition	second-class condition
first-class condition	simple condition
fourth-class condition	temporal clause
less-probable future condition	third-class condition

For Further Reading

Robertson 950–1049
Dana and Mantey 269–303
BDF 239–56
Wallace 656–725

14

To Koine Phrase

The Greek of the New Testament

S tarting in May of 334 B.C., Alexander, the 22-year-old king of Macedon, led his victorious army through four pitched battles, two sieges, and innumerable smaller engagements that enabled him to conquer territory that now goes under the names of Turkey, Syria, Lebanon, Palestine, Israel, Egypt, Iraq, Iran, and Afghanistan. Reaching the banks of the Beas River in Pakistan, he reluctantly turned back as his exhausted troops threatened mutiny. Three years later, in 323 B.C., he died in Babylon, just as he was planning an expedition all the way from Egypt along the North African coast to the Atlantic.

Historians agree about the magnitude of his conquests and about one of its most important effects: the establishment of a city-based Greek colonial aristocracy that imposed its culture on the native peoples in what we know today as the Middle East. But about the motives and character of the young man who carried out this tremendous enterprise there has been continual controversy. On the one hand, he has been credited with a belief in and a policy of establishing "the brotherhood of mankind." On the other hand, his expedition has been dismissed as utter folly, and scholars have compared him to a young Nazi let loose on the world, a visionary megalomaniac serving the needs of his own all-consuming ego.

In his short lifetime he defied the limits set on human achievement by the gods; after his death, he became the stuff of legend. Contrary to popular belief, Alexander did not burn the Persian king's great palace

147

at Persepolis during a drunken stupor. He did indeed burn the palace, but it was in retaliation for the Persian's desecration of Greek temples during the Persian invasion of Greece, not as the result of a drunken escapade. On the other hand, the story of his taming of the wild horse Bucephalus, the horse he later rode all the way to Pakistan, is based on solid historical evidence.

There is, however, one aspect of Alexander's saga on which all historians are in agreement: he had, as has been said of the Germans, a genius for warfare. From childhood he had been trained for it as a member of the corps of royal pages. Later, at the ripe old age of sixteen, he suppressed a tribal revolt in Macedon while his father Philip campaigned abroad. Two years later he led the famous cavalry charge that delivered the decisive blow to the Greek forces at Chaeronea, thus making Philip the master of Greece. And at the age of twenty-two, now king after Philip's assassination, he moved with astounding speed to defeat the Getae on the Danube far to the north and then swept south to suppress a revolt of the Greek cities led by the city of Thebes, which he destroyed. In the great pitched battles that followed, in a swift maneuver through the awesome mountains of Afghanistan, and in the complicated siege operations at Tyre and Gaza, his courage in the vanguard of his troops (he was wounded six times) made him ἀνίκητος, "invincible," the word the Sibyl at Delphi screamed at him and which he adopted as an official title.

After the defeat of the Persian king's last army at Gaugamela in 331 in what is now Iraq, and after the death of Darius shortly afterward, Alexander faced a crucial choice between two policies. He could have called a halt there and established a defensible frontier that gave him control of the most fertile areas of the Persian Empire. Instead, he chose to press on into unknown and fearsomely difficult terrain, most of it mountain or desert. This decision was partly the result of his belief that the gods had decreed that he would be king of all Asia. He had been taught by his tutor Aristotle that the land mass of Asia met the encircling ocean not far east of where he was. Yet the sober political reality was that he and his Macedonians, in an age when communications were no faster than a horse could ride, could never effectively govern an empire as large as the one he had acquired. So he appointed more and more high-ranking Persian officials to positions of influence on his staff, encouraged intermarriage between Macedonians and Persians, and instituted a program for training Persian boys for eventual service in the army. Measures such as these did not sit well with some of his older generals, and growing resentment fueled conspiracies against him.

When Alexander died, his empire broke up into separate kingdoms headed by his disgruntled generals. But he had changed the world. In the old, now liberated cities of Asia Minor—Ephesus and Pergamum—

as well as in the newly founded cities of the Middle East—Antioch and Alexandria—the culture and language of the colonial aristocracy was Greek. When three centuries after Alexander's death the life and teachings of Jesus of Nazareth were written down, the language used was not Jesus' native Aramaic but Greek, which, thanks to Alexander's conquests, had become the cultural lingua franca of the Mediterranean world.

The Language of the New Testament

It would be outside the province of this book to discuss the detailed development of the Greek language from Homeric to modern Greek, but the lesson is plain that Greek, as it spread over the civilized world, developed into a language of abiding importance. The conclusion now universally accepted by philologists is that the Greek of the New Testament, in all essential respects, is the vernacular Koine of the first century A.D., the common language of the Roman imperial period.

Koine (κοινή) means "common" in the sense of pertaining to the public at large. Hence Koine Greek means the language commonly spoken everywhere—the basic means of communication of people throughout the Roman Empire. This dialect was basically the late Attic vernacular, spoken in Athens, with dialectical and provincial influences. The Koine has left, in addition to the Greek New Testament, other literary monuments that are invaluable sources of light on the sacred text, including the papyri, inscriptions, and above all the Septuagint, the ancient version of the Old Testament that became the Bible of the early church and was used extensively by the New Testament writers.

Koine Greek itself exhibits three important characteristics. The first, semantic change, is a natural feature of any living language. Often certain words simply weakened their meaning in the Koine period. For example, the verb λαλέω meant *babble* in Classical Greek, but in the New Testament it appears as the ordinary word for *speak*. In the New Testament the preposition εἰς can mean *in* as well as *into*. The conjunction ἵνα, as we have seen, has a much wider meaning than *in order that* (it is often used in content clauses). The tendency to use the comparative degree of the adjective for the superlative has also been noted.

In the second place, Koine Greek exhibits greater simplicity than Classical Greek. This is seen particularly in the composition of its sentences, which tend toward coordination rather than subordination of clauses. In morphology it has a clear tendency toward simplification. This is perhaps most noticeable in the fact that the old μι-verbs are steadily being replaced by ω-verbs (e.g., δεικνύω is competing with δείκνυμι). In addition, periphrastic tenses are on the rise, and the optative mood is disappearing. The future tense of infinitives and participles hardly occurs at all.

Finally, Koine Greek shows unmistakable traces of a tendency toward more explicit (some would say more redundant) expression. We see a preference for compound verbs over simplex verbs, the use of pronouns as subjects of verbs, the use of prepositional phrases to replace simple cases, a preference for ἵνα instead of the infinitive, and the use of direct rather than indirect discourse. Adverbs abound, as do parenthetical statements and emphatic expressions such as *each and every* and *the very same*.

For the most part, the men who wrote the New Testament employed this common language, and students of the New Testament would do well to study its characteristics in detail. Like a new alloy, the Koine powerfully blended together the various Greek dialects into a single language used by Greeks as well as non-Greeks. Even those who held tenaciously to their native tongues, like the Egyptians, knew Greek.

At the same time, Koine Greek was not entirely uniform. Various literary levels existed, depending on the writer's background or education. In the first century A.D. some writers even attempted to turn the clock back by advocating a return to the old classical form of Greek, decrying the Koine as a debased form of the language. The artificial style they produced (called "Atticistic" Greek) contrasted with the dialect of everyday life.

The New Testament itself reveals several styles of Greek among its authors. The Epistle to the Hebrews, with its careful progression of argument and elevated diction, lies at one extreme. Luke and Acts also reveal good, literary style, though the author is able to vary his style considerably (cf. the colloquial Greek of Peter's speech in Acts 15:7–11 with the rhetorical nature of Paul's Areopagus speech in Acts 17:22–31). Paul's Greek is more or less colloquial, but that may be partly due to his amanuenses, the secretaries who wrote from his dictation. At the other end of the spectrum lies the grammar of Revelation, which reflects the work of a Semitic-speaking person who is just learning Greek (though many of the idioms he uses have parallels in colloquial papyri texts).

New Testament Semitisms

The special case of Revelation raises the larger issue of possible Semitic influences in the language of the Greek New Testament. No one who knows Hebrew or another Semitic language could fail to be impressed by the Semitic tone and flavor of the New Testament and by its adoption of Semitic modes of speech. For example, the expression "he opened his mouth" at the beginning of the Sermon on the Mount (Matt. 5:2) cannot be interpreted solely in the light of Greek grammar but must also be read in the light of Semitic language patterns, since the phrase indicates the beginning of some profound or solemn pronouncement (cf. Job 3:1). Another example is the very common ἀποκριθεὶς εἶπεν, "answering, he said." No Greek person of any period would say or write ἀποκριθεὶς εἶπεν any more than you or I would say "He answered and said" unless we were seeking to imitate biblical language. These are but two indications that the New Testament cannot be interpreted solely in terms of Greek grammar but must also be studied in terms of its Semitic background.

The occurrence of Semitisms in the New Testament can be attributed to four basic causes. First, by the time the New Testament was written, Koine Greek had already absorbed many Semitic words and idioms that were in use by Greek writers who knew no Hebrew or any other Semitic language. Second, all the New Testament writers, with the possible exception of Luke, were Jews whose usual language of speech was Aramaic or Hebrew and who had a considerable knowledge of the Hebrew Bible. Third, these writers consciously modeled themselves after the style of the Greek version of the Old Testament, the Septuagint, which often gives a literal translation of the original Hebrew. Finally, it is possible that the New Testament writers incorporated oral or written sources that were translations of Aramaic or Hebrew into Greek and that contained Semitisms in proportion to the literalness of the translation. Thus, it would be surprising if speakers whose linguistic background was Semitic did not betray some Semitic influence in their use of Greek.

The most common Semitisms are the following:[1]

- *Word order.* In Semitic languages the verb tends to come first in a sentence or clause, and this tendency is also found in the New Testament (see Luke 1:51–55; 1 Tim. 3:16).
- *Asyndeton.* The absence of a conjunction where one might be expected is a feature that is contrary to the nature of the Greek language. Most Greek sentences are linked by a connecting particle and asyndeton is generally used for rhetorical effect (see Acts 20:17–35). The frequent use of asyndeton in the Fourth Gospel (see, for instance, John 5:3) is best explained as the result of Semitic influence.
- *Coordination of clauses.* In Classical Greek, sentences usually contained one main verb; all other verbs tended to be subordinated in adverbial clauses of one kind or another. Hebrew, on the other hand, tended to place main verbs side by side, joining them together

---

1. For further discussion, see my "New Testament Semitisms," *Bible Translator* 39 (1988): 215–23.

with a simple conjunction (*waw*, and). The constantly recurring *and* (καί) of the Gospels is certainly Semitic in flavor. This type of construction is most characteristic of the Gospel of Mark, which has only a single instance of a longer Greek sentence with subordinating participles (see Mark 5:25–27).

- *Redundant pronouns.* The Hebrew relative pronoun is indeclinable and genderless and therefore requires a personal pronoun in the clause that follows. This has influenced a few New Testament passages in which an unnecessary pronoun appears after a relative pronoun (see, for example, Mark 7:25).

- *Redundant use of prepositions.* A characteristic feature of Semitic usage is the repetition of a preposition before every noun of a series that it governs. Such a construction is intolerable in literary Greek, but it occurs no less than eleven times in Mark alone (see, for example, Mark 3:7–8; 6:56; 11:1).

- *The use of the positive adjective for the comparative or superlative.* Semitic languages, with the exception of Arabic, have no special forms for the comparative and superlative adjectives. Instead, the positive adjective is used, as reflected, for example, in Mark 9:43: "If your hand causes you to stumble, cut it off; it is *better* (καλόν, good) for you to enter life crippled than to have your two hands and to go to hell."

- *Redundant use of "saying."* Indirect speech is unknown in biblical Hebrew. All speech is recorded directly, whether the words recorded were the actual words spoken or represent the general meaning of what was said. The Hebrew word most closely corresponding to the Greek participle λέγων (saying) is used to introduce a quotation. This idiom is well illustrated in Mark 8:28: "And they said to him, *saying.* . . ." For other examples, see Matthew 23:1–2; 28:18; Luke 14:3; 24:6–7.

- *Introductory ἐγένετο.* The peculiar use of the Greek verb ἐγένετο with another verb often reproduces a closely corresponding Semitic idiom meaning *so it was* or *it came to pass.* This Semitism appears far more frequently in Luke's writings than anywhere else (Mark has only four instances). An example is Luke 2:6: "And *so it was,* while they were there, the days were completed for her to give birth."

- *Future indicative used as an imperative.* The Hebrew verb form most closely corresponding to the Greek future indicative is often used to express commands. This construction has probably influenced a passage like Mark 9:35: "Whoever wants to be first, *he will be* last [= *he must be* last]."

- *The use of ἰδού.* The particle ἰδού (behold) is often used in the New Testament in imitation of the corresponding Hebrew expression (see Matt. 1:20; 2:9; 3:16; Luke 1:20, 31, 36; Acts 12:7; James 5:9).
- *The meaning of words.* Probably the most important influence exerted by the Semitic languages on New Testament Greek is found in the meaning of certain theological and ethical terms. One example is the Greek word νόμος, which is usually translated *law.* The basic meaning of the word in Greek is *custom* or *convention,* for the Greeks held that law was simply codified custom. But in the Septuagint the word is used as the equivalent of the Hebrew term *torah,* which means *instruction* and was applied to the Books of Moses, or the Law. Thus, when the New Testament writers wished to speak of law, not in the sense of human convention but in the sense of God's revealed will, the noun νόμος lay ready at hand. Much the same happened with a number of other words, including names and titles of divine beings, psychological terms, and words denoting such theological concepts as righteousness, mercy, sin, atonement, sacrifice, propitiation, and reconciliation. Thus the meaning of many significant words in the New Testament cannot be found in the ordinary Greek dictionary but must be sought against the background of the Hebrew Old Testament and its Greek translation, the Septuagint.

Conclusion

Flying into Rome one day, the thought occurred to me that our Italian captain, piloting an Alitalia jetliner that was landing at Da Vinci Airport, was required by international law to speak, not Italian, but English with the tower.

Similarly, two thousand years ago Greek was the lingua franca of the civilized world, the medium through which the apostles could communicate their message across the length and breadth of the Mediterranean regions. Who but Providence could have enabled the apostles to carry the message of Christ in one language and be understood wherever they went? The conquests of Alexander had, it seems, a divine purpose after all.

For Further Reading

Robertson 49–139
Dana and Mantey 1–15
BDF 1–6
Zerwick 161–64
Wallace 12–30

Postscript

You would not have come this far with me if you weren't reasonably interested in Greek grammar. Doubtless you will catch yourself in an occasional weak moment, the kind all flesh is heir to, and wonder if it was worth all the trouble. Later, as you begin to unearth the treasures in your Greek New Testament, you will be glad you paused to mull over the examples that litter this book. But though you may actually end up enjoying Greek, you should do so without self-consciousness or you will become pretentious and silly. You would then be like a horse with a broken leg: out of kindness, you should be shot.

Studies indicate that a knowledge of Greek grammar may be helpful to one's preaching, that it may help one study better, organize sermons better, and think more clearly about a biblical passage. But be cautious about taking my word for this; the final evidence is not in. Errors in New Testament interpretation still sprout like dandelions in sermons and commentaries. Taken individually, none of them is necessarily calamitous, but too many dandelions signify a poorly tended lawn.

The most insidious error is to think that one has arrived. When Harvard presented Andrew Jackson with an honorary doctorate in 1833, Jackson had a small problem. His schooling was meager, and the ceremony was in Latin. To express his thanks, he thundered out all the Latin he knew: *"E pluribus unum,* my dear friends! *Sine qua non! Quid pro quo!"* Many pastors have been less honest with their audiences.

So you must keep on keeping on. As I said in the preface, there's always more. For starters, if you liked this book, read it again. Here are some other suggestions.

Acquire a good dictionary of New Testament Greek. An excellent investment is Walter Bauer, *A Greek-English Lexicon of the New Testament and Other Early Christian Literature,* a German import translated and adapted by William F. Arndt and F. Wilbur Gingrich (2d ed., rev. and augmented by F. Wilbur Gingrich and Frederick W. Danker;

Chicago: University of Chicago Press, 1979).[1] This standard New Testament lexicon may be supplemented by G. Abbott-Smith, *A Manual Greek Lexicon of the New Testament,* 3d ed. (Edinburgh: T. & T. Clark, 1937)—"manual" meaning that you can pick it up with one hand.

You will also want to acquire a compendious reference grammar, such as A. T. Robertson's massive *Grammar of the Greek New Testament in the Light of Historical Research* (Nashville: Broadman, 1934). For exegetical issues I strongly recommend Daniel B. Wallace, *Greek Grammar beyond the Basics* (Grand Rapids: Zondervan, 1996)—a book that, happily, goes way beyond the basics. Both tomes are good to browse in, and with a little patience and ingenuity you can generally find an answer to even the obscurest grammatical questions, accompanied by abundant illustrations.

For building a working vocabulary of New Testament Greek, a guide long treasured by students and teachers of Greek is Bruce M. Metzger, *Lexical Aids for Students of New Testament Greek,* 3d ed. (reprint, Grand Rapids: Baker, 1998). Among its useful features is the classification of words according to their roots. Warren C. Trenchard has refined and furthered this approach in *The Student's Complete Vocabulary Guide to the Greek New Testament* (Grand Rapids: Zondervan, 1992). It includes every common word that has a cognate affinity for another in the Greek New Testament. Of course, it also includes a section with words according to their frequency of occurrence.

What then? Two tracks deserve mention. The first involves exegesis, and here students are very well served indeed: see especially Gordon D. Fee, *New Testament Exegesis,* rev. ed. (Louisville: Westminster/John Knox, 1993); Walter L. Liefeld, *New Testament Exposition* (Grand Rapids: Zondervan, 1984); Neal Windham, *New Testament Greek for Preachers and Teachers* (Lanham, Md.: University Press of America, 1991); and David Alan Black, *Using New Testament Greek in Ministry* (Grand Rapids: Baker, 1993). These books may be used in conjunction with two standard textbooks on New Testament interpretation: I. Howard Marshall, ed., *New Testament Interpretation* (Grand Rapids: Eerdmans, 1977) and David Alan Black and David S. Dockery, eds., *New Testament Criticism and Interpretation* (Grand Rapids: Zondervan, 1991). On text-critical issues, the standard textbook is still Bruce M. Metzger, *The Text of the New Testament,* 3d ed. (Oxford: Oxford University Press, 1992), though a less technical alternative is David Alan Black, *New Testament Textual Criticism* (Grand Rapids: Baker, 1994).

The second track to pursue takes you into the world of linguistics via such works as Moisés Silva, *Biblical Words and Their Meaning: An Intro-*

---

1. A major revision of this work is scheduled for release in 1998–99.

duction to Lexical Semantics, rev. ed. (Grand Rapids: Zondervan, 1994); David Alan Black, *Linguistics for Students of New Testament Greek,* 2d ed. (Grand Rapids: Baker, 1995); and Peter Cotterell and Max Turner, *Linguistics and Biblical Interpretation* (Downers Grove, Ill.: InterVarsity, 1989). On the related topic of discourse analysis, see David Alan Black, ed., *Linguistics and New Testament Interpretation: Essays on Discourse Analysis* (Nashville: Broadman & Holman, 1992) and Stanley E. Porter and D. A. Carson, eds., *Discourse Analysis and Other Topics of Biblical Greek* (Sheffield: Sheffield Academic Press, 1995). (It may appear a bit self-serving to list here so many of my own writings on New Testament studies, but I assure you, dear reader, that all royalties I receive go directly to needy children.)[2]

In conclusion, I hope you enjoy your Greek studies, and that many years from now you will be able to say proudly and with deep satisfaction, "It's *still* Greek to me!"

2. My own.

Key to the Exercises

Chapter 1

1. The disciples hear the words of the prophets.
2. We remain with the brothers in the house according to the law.
3. You speak words against the law of the disciples and the prophets.
4. In the church we are learning the word of God.
5. The young men are teaching the children in the wilderness, Lord.
6. The apostles were writing the epistles on the Sabbath.
7. We were teaching the gospel to the children of the soldiers.
8. Now the crowds were eating the loaves in the wilderness and drinking the fruit of the vine.
9. Jesus himself was saving the sinners from sin.
10. The apostle sent the servant to your house.
11. For the disciples were fasting for forty days.
12. The servants themselves will send these books into that temple.
13. God sent angels so that they might preach to the crowds.
14. Do not forbid the little children to come to me.
15. Jesus said to her, "It is true that you do not have a husband. For you have had five husbands, and the one whom you now have is not your husband." The woman said to him, "Lord, I see that you are a prophet."

Chapter 2

See Phil. 1:9–11.

Chapter 3

See 1 Thess. 1:1–5.

Chapter 4

1. A servant is not greater than his master.
2. This woman is younger than her sister.

3. The weakness of God is stronger than people.
4. The sons of this age are wiser than the sons of light.
5. My Father is greater than all.
6. There are twelve months in a year.
7. I am the true vine, and my Father is the vinegrower.
8. These words are faithful and true.
9. Great is your faith.
10. The twelve were with Jesus in a certain city.
11. A certain man had two sons.
12. The body without the spirit is dead.
13. Great is the love of God.
14. Faithful is the saying.
15. He will be called great in the kingdom of heaven.
16. Many are the vessels of the temple.
17. Faith without works is dead.
18. Many blind people are in the road.
19. For this reason the sons of God are more blessed.

Chapter 5

1. These men were dying in the wilderness.
2. Therefore this man was a disciple of John.
3. These women were remaining in the boat.
4. For this was his commandment.
5. In that day the apostles were praising the wisdom of the Lord.
6. For he himself will save the people.
7. He was sending her from the temple.
8. These are her houses.
9. A certain man is saying this.
10. The one who is not with me is against me.
11. Which of the two did the father's will?
12. Then a certain woman came to him.
13. Lord, if you want to, order me to come to you.
14. You are a slave, but I am free.
15. They were wanting to hear the words that Jesus was speaking.
16. I order you to come out of the house.
17. The same angels will prepare themselves to go.
18. You will have life in yourselves.
19. Should I come to the same house?
20. Why are you baptizing if you are not the Christ?
21. Jesus said to her, "I am the resurrection and the life."
22. This woman was full of good works.
23. This cup is the new covenant.

24. How can anyone enter?
25. To what should I compare this generation?
26. This is my beloved Son, in whom I am well pleased.
27. We have fellowship with one another.
28. Now even our fellowship is with the Father and with the Son Jesus Christ.
29. All the women gave their father the same gift.
30. The Spirit himself bears witness with our spirit.
31. The man to whom I sent gifts is coming.
32. You did not choose me, but I chose you.
33. I have loved you.
34. Who sinned, this man or his parents?
35. Among you is standing one whom you do not know.
36. I appeal to you on behalf of my child, whom I bore in chains.
37. You are cut off from Christ, you who would be justified by the law.
38. By what authority are you doing these things?
39. How many loaves do you have?
40. If you are the Son of God, throw yourself down.
41. Pray for one another.
42. My judgment is just, because I do not seek my own will.

Chapter 6

1. But there are some of you who do not believe.
2. Now Martha was distracted by much service.
3. But perfect love casts out fear.
4. Everyone who believes in him will not be ashamed.
5. Blessed are the merciful, for they themselves will receive mercy.
6. For tomorrow will worry about itself.
7. For the word that is of the cross is foolishness to those who are perishing.
8. Consider the Apostle and High Priest of our confession.
9. But you denied the Holy and Righteous One.
10. Blessed is the one who keeps alert and preserves his garments.
11. Blessed are those who hunger and thirst after righteousness.
12. And this is the testimony of John.
13. And Elizabeth was filled with the Holy Spirit.
14. Abraham fathered Isaac, and Isaac fathered Jacob.
15. By the grace of God I am what I am.
16. You are to worship the Lord your God.
17. Let your light so shine before people.
18. The thief does not come except to steal, murder, and destroy.
19. I am the king of the Jews.

20. Are you, then, the Son of God?
21. I, Paul, wrote this with my own hand.
22. For God is my witness.
23. Now before faith came we were held as prisoners under the law.
24. They were marveling that he was staying so long in the temple.
25. And a scribe came forward and said to him, "Teacher, I will follow you."

Chapter 7

1. Now while walking beside the sea he saw two brothers.
2. Go in through the narrow gate.
3. For since by man there is death, there is also by man the resurrection of the dead.
4. And being warned in a dream not to return to Herod, they departed for their own country by another road.
5. Now I am not asking on behalf of these only.
6. Then after three years I went up to Jerusalem.
7. I was remaining daily with you, teaching in the temple.
8. If God is for us, who can be against us?
9. Do not judge according to appearance, but judge with righteous judgment.
10. And taking him aside from the crowd by himself, he put his fingers into his ears.
11. And the one who falls on this rock will be broken to pieces.
12. The crowds were amazed at his teaching.
13. If anyone preaches to you beyond what you received, let him be anathema.
14. For I too am a man under authority, having soldiers under me.
15. Therefore having been justified by faith, we have peace with God through the Lord Jesus Christ.

Chapter 9

1. The Lord judges the souls of people.
2. The church is faithful.
3. We are beloved children of God.
4. The first is last, and the last first.
5. You are holy, Lord.
6. We are calling the other young men.
7. We were preaching the gospel to the people.
8. God was sending his angels into the world.
9. Jesus himself was not baptizing, but his disciples were.
10. You are being sent by the teachers to another crowd.

11. After these things, the tax collectors were being taught by elders in the church.
12. We were going with the disciples to the sea.
13. The elders will have the sheep that are being saved from the enemies.
14. You will prophesy to this people, and they will obey you.
15. Should we hide the child in the house?
16. Sanctify yourselves, for the day of the Lord is near.
17. Let peace inhabit your hearts.
18. You sent the tax collectors to buy the garments.
19. He said that he saw the boats.
20. By this we know the love of God, because he sent his beloved Son into the world.
21. We knew that the disciples learned many things from the apostles.
22. But when the soldiers came into the house, they announced that Peter had sent them.
23. But Jesus said to the paralytic, "Get up, pick up your bed, and go into your house." And when he heard these things, he picked up the bed and departed.
24. The prophet said that all miracles are from God.
25. Jesus was led by the Spirit into the mountains to be tempted by the devil.
26. For by grace we were saved through the will of God.
27. And when the demon was cast out the crowd began to marvel, but many were saying that these miracles were not of God.
28. You were called fools by the wise of this age.
29. You have filled Jerusalem with your teaching.
30. God has spoken this through the mouth of all the prophets.
31. He came in order that he might testify about the light.
32. Whoever believes in the name of the Lord will be saved.
33. Therefore, should we say that we should do bad so that good might come?
34. You have a fine way of setting aside the commandment of God in order that you might keep your tradition!
35. Do not judge in order that you might not be judged.
36. Do not be afraid, but speak and do not be silent.

Chapter 10

1. The apostle came to see the people and to speak the word.
2. I have need to be baptized by you, but you are asking to be baptized by me?
3. In the kingdom you must become spiritual children.

4. I am not worthy to teach the disciple whom you sent.
5. We will make disciples of all the nations.
6. This is the hour of repentance. Therefore, it is time to repent.
7. Jesus came into the world to save sinners.
8. Because Jesus had healed their eyes, the blind believed in him.
9. Not to know the truth is evil.
10. Before the apostle began to preach the gospel, Jesus had already gone up to heaven.
11. Because Jesus had come into the house, his disciples began preaching.
12. After the slave preaches, we will lead the crowds to Jesus.
13. To love is good.
14. Jesus went to see the disciples.
15. They led him away to crucify him.
16. Put on the whole armor of God so that you can stand firm.
17. Your Father knows what you have need of before you ask him.
18. Come down before my child dies.
19. You cannot serve God and Mammon.
20. But I do not permit a woman to teach or to exercise authority over a man, but [I want her] to be silent.
21. It has been granted to you on behalf of Christ not only to believe in him, but also to suffer for him.
22. She is free to marry whom she wishes.
23. Let every man be quick to listen, slow to speak.
24. For he was about to die.
25. It is not lawful for you to pick up your mattress.
26. You think that you have eternal life in them.
27. Have the men sit down.
28. They heard that he had done this sign.
29. He must rise from the dead.
30. From that time, Jesus began to show his disciples that he would have to go to Jerusalem, suffer many things from the elders, high priests, and scribes, die, and on the third day be raised.

Chapter 11

1. Therefore, listen to the parable of the sower.
2. And he came preaching in their synagogues and casting out demons.
3. Behold, I see the heavens opened.
4. The word of God is living.
5. Those who had eaten the loaves were five thousand men.
6. But this is the will of him who sent me.

7. When the whole crowd saw him, they were completely amazed.
8. He went away grieving.
9. Let us labor, working with our own hands.
10. He emptied himself by taking the form of a servant.
11. We will reap if we do not lose heart.
12. Although they knew God, they did not glorify him as God.
13. He was saying this to signify by what kind of death he was about to die.
14. Go and show yourself to the priest.
15. When he saw that this was pleasing to the Jews, he intended to arrest Peter also.
16. Then Paul stretched forth his hand and began to give his defense.
17. But when Ananias heard these words, he fell down and breathed his last. And great fear came upon all those who heard.
18. Although he was a Son, he learned obedience from what he suffered.
19. For John came neither eating nor drinking, and you say, "He has a demon."
20. Not everyone who says to me, "Lord, Lord," is good, but the one who does the will of my Father in heaven [is].
21. For he was teaching them as having authority, and not as their scribes.
22. Now while Peter was still saying these words, the Holy Spirit fell on all those who heard the word.
23. Now when he saw the crowds, he went up on the mountain. After he sat down, his disciples came to him. Then he opened his mouth and began teaching them, saying, "Blessed are those who are poor in spirit, for theirs is the kingdom of heaven."

Chapter 12

See John 21:15–19.

Chapter 13

See Acts 1:1–5.

Appendix 1

Greek Verb Conjugations

Regular Omega Verbs

Using λύω (*I loose*, stem λυ-) as an example, here is the conjugation pattern for omega verbs.

First Principal Part

		Pres. Act.	**Pres. M./P.**	**Imperf. Act.**	**Imperf. M./P.**
Indic.	Sg. 1.	λύω	λύομαι	ἔλυον	ἐλυόμην
	2.	λύεις	λύῃ	ἔλυες	ἐλύου
	3.	λύει	λύεται	ἔλυε(ν)	ἐλύετο
	Pl. 1.	λύομεν	λυόμεθα	ἐλύομεν	ἐλυόμεθα
	2.	λύετε	λύεσθε	ἐλύετε	ἐλύεσθε
	3.	λύουσι(ν)	λύονται	ἔλυον	ἐλύοντο
Subj.	Sg. 1.	λύω	λύωμαι		
	2.	λύῃς	λύῃ		
	3.	λύῃ	λύηται		
	Pl. 1.	λύωμεν	λυώμεθα		
	2.	λύητε	λύησθε		
	3.	λύωσι(ν)	λύωνται		
Opt.	Sg. 1.	λύοιμι	λυοίμην		
	2.	λύοις	λύοιο		
	3.	λύοι	λύοιτο		
	Pl. 1.	λύοιμεν	λυοίμεθα		
	2.	λύοιτε	λύοισθε		
	3.	λύοιεν	λύοιντο		
Impv.	Sg. 2.	λῦε	λύου		
	3.	λυέτω	λυέσθω		
	Pl. 2.	λύετε	λύεσθε		
	3.	λυόντων or λυέτωσαν	λυέσθων or λυέσθωσαν		
Infin.		λύειν	λύεσθαι		

Part	Masc.	λύων	λυόμενος
	Fem.	λύουσα	λυομένη
	Neut.	λῦον	λυόμενον

Second and Third Principal Parts

		Fut. Act.	Fut. Mid.	Aor. Act.	Aor. Mid.
Indic.	Sg. 1.	λύσω	λύσομαι	ἔλυσα	ἐλυσάμην
	2.	λύσεις	λύσῃ	ἔλυσας	ἐλύσω
	3.	λύσει	λύσεται	ἔλυσε(ν)	ἐλύσατο
	Pl. 1.	λύσομεν	λυσόμεθα	ἐλύσαμεν	ἐλυσάμεθα
	2.	λύσετε	λύσεσθε	ἐλύσατε	ἐλύσασθε
	3.	λύσουσι(ν)	λύσονται	ἔλυσαν	ἐλύσαντο
Subj.	Sg. 1.			λύσω	λύσωμαι
	2.			λύσῃς	λύσῃ
	3.			λύσῃ	λύσηται
	Pl. 1.			λύσωμεν	λυσώμεθα
	2.			λύσητε	λύσησθε
	3.			λύσωσι(ν)	λύσωνται
Opt.	Sg. 1.	λύσοιμι	λυσοίμην	λύσαιμι	λυσαίμην
	2.	λύσοις	λύσοιο	λύσαις	λύσαιο
	3.	λύσοι	λύσοιτο	λύσαι	λύσαιτο
	Pl. 1.	λύσοιμεν	λυσοίμεθα	λύσαιμεν	λυσαίμεθα
	2.	λύσοιτε	λύσοισθε	λύσαιτε	λύσαισθε
	3.	λύσοιεν	λύσοιντο	λύσαιεν	λύσαιντο
Impv.	Sg. 2.			λῦσον	λῦσαι
	3.			λυσάτω	λυσάσθω
	Pl. 2.			λύσατε	λύσασθε
	3.			λυσάντων or	λυσάσθων or
				λυσάτωσαν	λυσάσθωσαν
Infin.		λύσειν	λύσεσθαι	λῦσαι	λύσασθαι
Part.	Masc.	λύσων	λυσόμενος	λύσας	λυσάμενος
	Fem.	λύσουσα	λυσομένη	λύσασα	λυσαμένη
	Neut.	λῦσον	λυσόμενον	λῦσαν	λυσάμενον

Since λύω does not have a second aorist form, λείπω (*I leave*) is used to illustrate this conjugation pattern for the regular omega verb.

		2d Aor. Act.	2d Aor. Mid.
Indic.	Sg. 1.	ἔλιπον	ἐλιπόμην
	2.	ἔλιπες	ἐλίπου
	3.	ἔλιπε(ν)	ἐλίπετο
	Pl. 1.	ἐλίπομεν	ἐλιπόμεθα
	2.	ἐλίπετε	ἐλίπεσθε
	3.	ἔλιπον	ἐλίποντο
Subj.	Sg. 1.	λίπω	λίπωμαι
	2.	λίπῃς	λίπῃ
	3.	λίπῃ	λίπηται
	Pl. 1.	λίπωμεν	λιπώμεθα

	2.	λίπητε	λίπησθε
	3.	λίπωσι(ν)	λίπωνται

Opt.	Sg. 1.	λίποιμι	λιποίμην
	2.	λίποις	λίποιο
	3.	λίποι	λίποιτο
	Pl. 1.	λίποιμεν	λιποίμεθα
	2.	λίποιτε	λίποισθε
	3.	λίποιεν	λίποιντο

Impv.	Sg. 2.	λίπε	λιποῦ
	3.	λιπέτω	λιπέσθω
	Pl. 2.	λίπετε	λίπεσθε
	3.	λιπόντων	λιπέσθων
		or λιπέτωσαν	or λιπέσθωσαν

Infin.		λιπεῖν	λιπέσθαι

Part.	Masc.	λιπών	λιπόμενος
	Fem.	λιποῦσα	λιπομένη
	Neut.	λιπόν	λιπόμενον

Fourth Principal Part

Between the perfect and pluperfect active forms of λύω, the verb λείπω is used to illustrate the second perfect active conjugation pattern for the regular omega verb.

		Perf. Act.	2d Perf. Act.	Plup. Act.
Indic.	Sg. 1.	λέλυκα	λέλοιπα	ἐλελύκειν
	2.	λέλυκας	λέλοιπας	ἐλελύκεις
	3.	λέλυκε(ν)	λέλοιπε(ν)	ἐλελύκει
	Pl. 1.	λελύκαμεν	λελοίπαμεν	ἐλελύκειμεν
	2.	λελύκατε	λελοίπατε	ἐλελύκειτε
	3.	λελύκασι(ν)	λελοίπασι(ν)	ἐλελύκεισαν
		or λέλυκαν		

Subj.	Sg. 1.	λελύκω		λελοίπω
	2.	λελύκῃς		λελοίπῃς
	3.	λελύκῃ		λελοίπῃ
	Pl. 1.	λελύκωμεν		λελοίπωμεν
	2.	λελύκητε		λελοίπητε
	3.	λελύκωσι(ν)		λελοίπωσι(ν)

Opt.	Sg. 1.	λελύκοιμι		λελοίποιμι
	2.	λελύκοις		λελοίποις
	3.	λελύκοι		λελοίποι
	Pl. 1.	λελύκοιμεν		λελοίποιμεν
	2.	λελύκοιτε		λελοίποιτε
	3.	λελύκοιεν		λελοίποιεν

Infin.		λελυκέναι		λελοιπέναι

Part.	Masc.	λελυκώς		λελοιπώς
	Fem.	λελυκυῖα		λελοιπυῖα
	Neut.	λελυκός		λελοιπός

Fifth Principal Part

			Perf. M./P.	Plup. M./P.	Fut. Perf. Pass.
Indic.	Sg.	1.	λέλυμαι	ἐλελύμην	λελύσομαι
		2.	λέλυσαι	ἐλέλυσο	λελύσῃ
		3.	λέλυται	ἐλέλυτο	λελύσεται
	Pl.	1.	λελύμεθα	ἐλελύμεθα	λελυσόμεθα
		2.	λέλυσθε	ἐλέλυσθε	λελύσεσθε
		3.	λέλυνται	ἐλέλυντο	λελύσονται
Subj.	Sg.	1.	λελυμένος ὦ		
		2.	λελυμένος ᾖς		
		3.	λελυμένος ᾖ		
	Pl.	1.	λελυμένοι ὦμεν		
		2.	λελυμένοι ἦτε		
		3.	λελυμένοι ὦσι(ν)		
Opt.	Sg.	1.	λελυμένος εἴην		λελυσοίμην
		2.	λελυμένος εἴης		λελύσοιο
		3.	λελυμένος εἴη		λελύσοιτο
	Pl.	1.	λελυμένοι εἴημεν		λελυσοίμεθα
		2.	λελυμένοι εἴητε		λελύσοισθε
		3.	λελυμένοι εἴησαν		λελύσοιντο
Infin.			λελύσθαι		λελύσεσθαι
Part.	Masc.		λελυμένος		λελυσόμενος
	Fem.		λελυμένη		λελυσομένη
	Neut.		λελυμένον		λελυσόμενον

Sixth Principal Part

Alongside the passive forms of λύω, the verb γράφω is used to illustrate the second aorist passive conjugation pattern for the regular omega verb.

			Fut. Pass.	Aor. Pass.	2d Aor. Pass.
Indic.	Sg.	1.	λυθήσομαι	ἐλύθην	ἐγράφην
		2.	λυθήσῃ	ἐλύθης	ἐγράφης
		3.	λυθήσεται	ἐλύθη	ἐγράφη
	Pl.	1.	λυθησόμεθα	ἐλύθημεν	ἐγράφημεν
		2.	λυθήσεσθε	ἐλύθητε	ἐγράφητε
		3.	λυθήσονται	ἐλύθησαν	ἐγράφησαν
Subj.	Sg.	1.		λυθῶ	γραφῶ
		2.		λυθῇς	γραφῇς
		3.		λυθῇ	γραφῇ
	Pl.	1.		λυθῶμεν	γραφῶμεν
		2.		λυθῆτε	γραφῆτε
		3.		λυθῶσι(ν)	γραφῶσι(ν)
Opt.	Sg.	1.	λυθησοίμην	λυθείην	γραφείην
		2.	λυθήσοιο	λυθείης	γραφείης
		3.	λυθήσοιτο	λυθείη	γραφείη
	Pl.	1.	λυθησοίμεθα	λυθείημεν	γραφείημεν
		2.	λυθήσοισθε	λυθείητε	γραφείητε
		3.	λυθήσοιντο	λυθείησαν	γραφείησαν

Impv.	Sg. 2.		λύθητι	γράφηθι
	3.		λυθήτω	γραφήτω
	Pl. 2.		λύθητε	γράφητε
	3.		λυθέντων or	γραφέντων or
			λυθήτωσαν	γραφήτωσαν
Infin.		λυθήσεσθαι	λυθῆναι	γραφῆναι
Part.	Masc.	λυθησόμενος	λυθείς	γραφείς
	Fem.	λυθησομένη	λυθεῖσα	γραφεῖσα
	Neut.	λυθησόμενον	λυθέν	γραφέν

Contract Verbs

Contract verbs come in three flavors: those with stems ending in α, ε, or o. These final vowels contract with the standard suffixes of the omega verb and create some interesting-looking endings. The verbs τιμάω (*I honor*, stem τιμα-), φιλέω (*I love*, stem φιλε-), and δηλόω (*I show*, stem δηλο-) are used as examples. In the future, aorist, and perfect tenses these verbs are formed like regular omega verbs because the intervening consonant prevents contraction (i.e., σ in the future and aorist; κ in the perfect). Therefore, only the present and imperfect tenses are given below. The forms in parentheses show the two vowels prior to contraction; next to them are the contracted forms, showing how the words would actually look in a Greek text.

Τιμάω

		Pres. Act.		Pres. Mid./Pass.	
Indic.	Sg. 1.	(τιμάω)	τιμῶ	(τιμάομαι)	τιμῶμαι
	2.	(τιμάεις)	τιμᾷς	(τιμάῃ)	τιμᾷ
	3.	(τιμάει)	τιμᾷ	(τιμάεται)	τιμᾶται
	Pl. 1.	(τιμάομεν)	τιμῶμεν	(τιμαόμεθα)	τιμώμεθα
	2.	(τιμάετε)	τιμᾶτε	(τιμάεσθε)	τιμᾶσθε
	3.	(τιμάουσι[ν])	τιμῶσι(ν)	(τιμάονται)	τιμῶνται
Subj.	Sg. 1.	(τιμάω)	τιμῶ	(τιμάωμαι)	τιμῶμαι
	2.	(τιμάῃς)	τιμᾷς	(τιμάῃ)	τιμᾷ
	3.	(τιμάῃ)	τιμᾷ	(τιμάηται)	τιμᾶται
	Pl. 1.	(τιμάωμεν)	τιμῶμεν	(τιμαώμεθα)	τιμώμεθα
	2.	(τιμάητε)	τιμᾶτε	(τιμάησθε)	τιμᾶσθε
	3.	(τιμάωσι[ν])	τιμῶσι(ν)	(τιμάωνται)	τιμῶνται
Impv.	Sg. 2.	(τίμαε)	τίμα	(τιμάου)	τιμῶ
	3.	(τιμαέτω)	τιμάτω	(τιμαέσθω)	τιμάσθω
	Pl. 2.	(τιμάετε)	τιμᾶτε	(τιμάεσθε)	τιμᾶσθε
	3.	(τιμαόντων)	τιμώντων	(τιμαέσθων) or	τιμάσθων or
		or (τιμαέτωσαν)	or τιμάτωσαν	(τιμαέσθωσαν)	τιμάσθωσαν
Infin.		(τιμάειν)	τιμᾶν	(τιμάεσθαι)	τιμᾶσθαι
Part.	Masc.	(τιμάων)	τιμῶν	(τιμαόμενος)	τιμώμενος
	Fem.	(τιμάουσα)	τιμῶσα	(τιμαομένη)	τιμωμένη
	Neut.	(τιμάον)	τιμῶν	(τιμαόμενον)	τιμώμενον

		Imperf. Act.		**Imperf. Mid./Pass.**	
Indic.	Sg. 1.	(ἐτίμαον)	ἐτίμων	(ἐτιμαόμην)	ἐτιμώμην
	2.	(ἐτίμαες)	ἐτίμας	(ἐτιμάου)	ἐτιμῶ
	3.	(ἐτίμαε)	ἐτίμα	(ἐτιμάετο)	ἐτιμᾶτο
	Pl. 1.	(ἐτιμάομεν)	ἐτιμῶμεν	(ἐτιμαόμεθα)	ἐτιμώμεθα
	2.	(ἐτιμάετε)	ἐτιμᾶτε	(ἐτιμάεσθε)	ἐτιμᾶσθε
	3.	(ἐτίμαον)	ἐτίμων	(ἐτιμάοντο)	ἐτιμῶντο

Φιλέω

		Pres. Act.		**Pres. Mid./Pass.**	
Indic.	Sg. 1.	(φιλέω)	φιλῶ	(φιλέομαι)	φιλοῦμαι
	2.	(φιλέεις)	φιλωεῖς	(φιλέῃ)	φιλῇ
	3.	(φιλέει)	φιλεῖ	(φιλέεται)	φιλεῖται
	Pl. 1.	(φιλέομεν)	φιλοῦμεν	(φιλεόμεθα)	φιλούμεθα
	2.	(φιλέετε)	φιλεῖτε	(φιλέεσθε)	φιλεῖσθε
	3.	(φιλέουσι[ν])	φιλοῦσι(ν)	(φιλέονται)	φιλοῦνται
Subj.	Sg. 1.	(φιλέω)	φιλῶ	(φιλέωμαι)	φιλῶμαι
	2.	(φιλέῃς)	φιλῇς	(φιλέῃ)	φιλῇ
	3.	(φιλέῃ)	φιλῇ	(φιλέηται)	φιλῆται
	Pl. 1.	(φιλέωμεν)	φιλῶμεν	(φιλεώμεθα)	φιλώμεθα
	2.	(φιλέητε)	φιλῆτε	(φιλέησθε)	φιλῆσθε
	3.	(φιλέωσι[ν])	φιλῶσι(ν)	(φιλέωνται)	φιλῶνται
Impv.	Sg. 2.	(φίλεε)	φίλει	(φιλέου)	φιλοῦ
	3.	(φιλεέτω)	φιλείτω	(φιλεέσθω)	φιλείσθω
	Pl. 2.	(φιλέετε)	φιλεῖτε	(φιλέεσθε)	φιλεῖσθε
	3.	(φιλεόντων) or	φιλούντων or	(φιλεέσθων) or	φιλείσθων or
		(φιλεέτωσαν)	φιλείτωσαν	(φιλεέσθωσαν)	φιλείσθωσαν
Infin.		(φιλέειν)	φιλεῖν	(φιλέεσθαι)	φιλεῖσθαι
Part.	Masc.	(φιλέων)	φιλῶν	(φιλεόμενος)	φιλούμενος
	Fem.	(φιλέουσα)	φιλοῦσα	(φιλεομένη)	φιλουμένη
	Neut.	(φιλέον)	φιλοῦν	(φιλεόμενον)	φιλούμενον

		Imperf. Act.		**Imperf. Mid./Pass.**	
Indic.	Sg. 1.	(ἐφίλεον)	ἐφίλουν	(ἐφιλεόμην)	ἐφιλούμην
	2.	(ἐφίλεες)	ἐφίλεις	(ἐφιλέου)	ἐφιλοῦ
	3.	(ἐφίλεε)	ἐφίλει	(ἐφιλέετο)	ἐφιλεῖτο
	Pl. 1.	(ἐφιλέομεν)	ἐφιλοῦμεν	(ἐφιλεόμεθα)	ἐφιλούμεθα
	2.	(ἐφιλέετε)	ἐφιλεῖτε	(ἐφιλέεσθε)	ἐφιλεῖσθε
	3.	(ἐφίλεον)	ἐφίλουν	(ἐφιλέοντο)	ἐφιλοῦντο

Δηλόω

		Pres. Act.		**Pres. Mid./Pass.**	
Indic.	Sg. 1.	(δηλόω)	δηλῶ	(δηλόομαι)	δηλοῦμαι
	2.	(δηλόεις)	δηλοῖς	(δηλόῃ)	δηλοῖ
	3.	(δηλόει)	δηλοῖ	(δηλόεται)	δηλοῦται
	Pl. 1.	(δηλόομεν)	δηλοῦμεν	(δηλοόμεθα)	δηλούμεθα

		2.	(δηλόετε)	δηλοῦτε	(δηλόεσθε)	δηλοῦσθε
		3.	(δηλόουσι[ν])	δηλοῦσι(ν)	(δηλόονται)	δηλοῦνται
Subj.	Sg.	1.	(δηλόω)	δηλῶ	(δηλόωμαι)	δηλῶμαι
		2.	(δηλόῃς)	δηλοῖς	(δηλόῃ)	δηλοῖ
		3.	(δηλόῃ)	δηλοῖ	(δηλόηται)	δηλῶται
	Pl.	1.	(δηλόωμεν)	δηλῶμεν	(δηλοώμεθα)	δηλώμεθα
		2.	(δηλόητε)	δηλῶτε	(δηλόησθε)	δηλῶσθε
		3.	(δηλόωσι[ν])	δηλῶσι(ν)	(δηλόωνται)	δηλῶνται
Impv.	Sg.	2.	(δήλοε)	δήλου	(δηλόου)	δηλοῦ
		3.	(δηλοέτω)	δηλούτω	(δηλοέσθω)	δηλούσθω
	Pl.	2.	(δηλόετε)	δηλοῦτε	(δηλόεσθε)	δηλοῦσθε
		3.	(δηλοόντων) or	δηλούντων or	(δηλοέσθων) or	δηλούσθων or
			(δηλοέτωσαν)	δηλούτωσαν	(δηλοέσθωσαν)	δηλούσθωσαν
Infin.			(δηλόειν)	δηλοῦν	(δηλόεσθαι)	δηλοῦσθαι
Part.	Masc.		(δηλόων)	δηλῶν	(δηλοόμενος)	δηλούμενος
	Fem.		(δηλόουσα)	δηλοῦσα	(δηλοομένη)	δηλουμένη
	Neut.		(δηλόον)	δηλοῦν	(δηλοόμενον)	δηλούμενον

			Imperf. Act.		**Imperf. Mid./Pass.**	
Indic.	Sg.	1.	(ἐδήλοον)	ἐδήλουν	(ἐδηλοόμην)	ἐδηλούμην
		2.	(ἐδήλοες)	ἐδήλους	(ἐδηλόου)	ἐδηλοῦ
		3.	(ἐδήλοε)	ἐδήλου	(ἐδηλόετο)	ἐδηλοῦτο
	Pl.	1.	(ἐδηλόομεν)	ἐδηλοῦμεν	(ἐδηλοόμεθα)	ἐδηλούμεθα
		2.	(ἐδηλόετε)	ἐδηλοῦτε	(ἐδηλόεσθε)	ἐδηλοῦσθε
		3.	(ἐδήλοον)	ἐδήλουν	(ἐδηλόοντο)	ἐδηλοῦντο

Liquid Verbs

Liquid verbs (verbs with stems ending in λ, μ, ν, or ρ) cannot take sigma when forming the future and aorist tenses (you try pronouncing λσ, μσ, νσ, or ρσ!). Except for the omission of σ these verbs take the standard suffixes of the omega verb, and their conjugation pattern looks similar to that of epsilon contract verbs. The verb κρίνω *(I judge)* is used below as an example.

			Fut. Act.	**Fut. Mid.**	**Fut. Pass.**
Indic.	Sg.	1.	κρινῶ	κρινοῦμαι	κρινήσομαι
		2.	κρινεῖς	κρινῇ	κρινήσῃ
		3.	κρινεῖ	κρινεῖται	κρινήσεται
	Pl.	1.	κρινοῦμεν	κρινούμεθα	κρινησόμεθα
		2.	κρινεῖτε	κρινεῖσθε	κρινήσεσθε
		3.	κρινοῦσι(ν)	κρινοῦνται	κρινήσονται
Infin.			κρινεῖν	κρινεῖσθαι	κρινήσεσθαι
Part.	Masc.		κρινῶν	κρινούμενος	κρινησόμενος
	Fem.		κρινοῦσα	κρινουμένη	κρινησομένη
	Neut.		κρινοῦν	κρινούμενον	κρινησόμενον

		Aor. Act.	Aor. Mid.	Aor. Pass.
Indic.	Sg. 1.	ἔκρινα	ἐκρινάμην	ἐκρίνην
	2.	ἔκρινας	ἐκρίνω	ἐκρίνης
	3.	ἔκρινε(ν)	ἐκρίνατο	ἐκρίνη
	Pl. 1.	ἐκρίναμεν	ἐκρινάμεθα	ἐκρίνημεν
	2.	ἐκρίνατε	ἐκρίνασθε	ἐκρίνητε
	3.	ἔκριναν	ἐκρίναντο	ἐκρίνησαν
Subj.	Sg. 1.	κρίνω	κρίνωμαι	κρινῶ
	2.	κρίνῃς	κρίνῃ	κρινῇς
	3.	κρίνῃ	κρίνηται	κρινῇ
	Pl. 1.	κρίνωμεν	κρινώμεθα	κρινῶμεν
	2.	κρίνητε	κρίνησθε	κρινῆτε
	3.	κρίνωσι(ν)	κρίνωνται	κρινῶσι(ν)
Impv.	Sg. 2.	κρῖνον	κρῖναι	κρίνηθι
	3.	κρινάτω	κρινάσθω	κρινήτω
	Pl. 2.	κρίνατε	κρίνασθε	κρίνητε
	3.	κρινάντων or	κρινάσθων or	κρινέντων or
		κρινάτωσαν	κρινάσθωσαν	κρινήτωσαν
Infin.		κρῖναι	κρίνασθαι	κρινῆναι
Part.	Masc.	κρίνας	κρινάμενος	κρινείς
	Fem.	κρίνασα	κριναμένη	κρινεῖσα
	Neut.	κρῖναν	κρινάμενον	κρινέν

Μι Verbs

Like contract verbs, the stems of these common μι verbs end in a vowel, which contracts with the verbal suffixes and creates some interesting-looking endings. However, unlike contract verbs, which take the standard suffixes of the omega verb, μι verbs use a different set of verbal suffixes. The table below shows the conjugation pattern for stems ending in α, ε, or ο. The verbs used to illustrate this conjugation pattern are ἵστημι (*I cause to stand, I set, I establish*, stem στα-), τίθημι (*I put, I place*, stem θε-), and δίδωμι (*I give*, stem δο-)—presented below in reverse order. Since these verbs form their futures and perfects like the omega verbs, only the present, imperfect, and aorist tenses are given. The verb of being, εἰμί *(I am)*, appears at the end of this series of conjugations.

Δίδωμι

		Pres. Act.	Pres. M./P.	Imperf. Act.	Imperf. M./P.
Indic.	Sg. 1.	δίδωμι	δίδομαι	ἐδίδουν	ἐδιδόμην
	2.	δίδως	δίδοσαι	ἐδίδους	ἐδίδοσο
	3.	δίδωσι(ν)	δίδοται	ἐδίδου	ἐδίδοτο
	Pl. 1.	δίδομεν	διδόμεθα	ἐδίδομεν	ἐδιδόμεθα
	2.	δίδοτε	δίδοσθε	ἐδίδοτε	ἐδίδοσθε
	3.	διδόασι(ν)	δίδονται	ἐδίδοσαν	ἐδίδοντο

Subj.	Sg. 1.	διδῶ	διδῶμαι
	2.	διδῷς	διδῷ
	3.	διδῷ	διδῶται
	Pl. 1.	διδῶμεν	διδώμεθα
	2.	διδῶτε	διδῶσθε
	3.	διδῶσι(ν)	διδῶνται

Impv.	Sg. 2.	δίδου	δίδοσο
	3.	διδότω	διδόσθω
	Pl. 2.	δίδοτε	δίδοσθε
	3.	διδόντων or	διδόσθων or
		διδότωσαν	διδόσθωσαν

Infin.		διδόναι	δίδοσθαι

Part.	Masc.	διδούς	διδόμενος
	Fem.	διδοῦσα	διδομένη
	Neut.	διδόν	διδόμενον

		Aor. Act.	**Aor. Mid.**	**Aor. Pass.**
Indic.	Sg. 1.	ἔδωκα	ἐδόμην	ἐδόθην
	2.	ἔδωκας	ἔδου	ἐδόθης
	3.	ἔδωκε(ν)	ἔδοτο	ἐδόθη
	Pl. 1.	ἐδώκαμεν	ἐδόμεθα	ἐδόθημεν
	2.	ἐδώκατε	ἔδοσθε	ἐδόθητε
	3.	ἔδωκαν	ἔδοντο	ἐδόθησαν

Subj.	Sg. 1.	δῶ	δῶμαι	δοθῶ
	2.	δῷς	δῷ	δοθῇς
	3.	δῷ	δῶται	δοθῇ
	Pl. 1.	δῶμεν	δώμεθα	δοθῶμεν
	2.	δῶτε	δῶσθε	δοθῆτε
	3.	δῶσι(ν)	δῶνται	δοθῶσι(ν)

Impv.	Sg. 2.	δός	δοῦ	δόθητι
	3.	δότω	δόσθω	δοθήτω
	Pl. 2.	δότε	δόσθε	δόθητε
	3.	δόντων or	δόσθων or	δοθέντων or
		δότωσαν	δόσθωσαν	δοθήτωσαν

Infin.		δοῦναι	δόσθαι	δοθῆναι

Part.	Masc.	δούς	δόμενος	δοθείς
	Fem.	δοῦσα	δομένη	δοθεῖσα
	Neut.	δόν	δόμενον	δοθέν

Τίθημι

		Pres. Act.	**Pres. M./P.**	**Imperf. Act.**	**Imperf. M./P.**
Indic.	Sg. 1.	τίθημι	τίθεμαι	ἐτίθην	ἐτιθέμην
	2.	τίθης	τίθεσαι	ἐτίθεις	ἐτίθεσο
	3.	τίθησι(ν)	τίθεται	ἐτίθει	ἐτίθετο
	Pl. 1.	τίθεμεν	τιθέμεθα	ἐτίθεμεν	ἐτιθέμεθα
	2.	τίθετε	τίθεσθε	ἐτίθετε	ἐτίθεσθε
	3.	τιθέασι(ν)	τίθενται	ἐτίθεσαν	ἐτίθεντο

Subj. Sg. 1.   τιθῶ   τιθῶμαι
       2.   τιθῇς   τιθῇ
       3.   τιθῇ   τιθῆται
       Pl. 1.   τιθῶμεν   τιθώμεθα
       2.   τιθῆτε   τιθῆσθε
       3.   τιθῶσι(ν)   τιθῶνται

Impv. Sg. 2.   τίθει   τίθεσο
       3.   τιθέτω   τιθέσθω
       Pl. 2.   τίθετε   τίθεσθε
       3.   τιθέντων or   τιθέσθων or
                   τιθέτωσαν   τιθέσθωσαν

Infin.   τιθέναι   τίθεσθαι

Part. Masc.   τιθείς   τιθέμενος
       Fem.   τιθεῖσα   τιθεμένη
       Neut.   τιθέν   τιθέμενον

		Aor. Act.	**Aor. Mid.**	**Aor. Pass.**
Indic.	Sg. 1.	ἔθηκα	ἐθέμην	ἐτέθην
	2.	ἔθηκας	ἔθου	ἐτέθης
	3.	ἔθηκε(ν)	ἔθετο	ἐτέθη
	Pl. 1.	ἐθήκαμεν	ἐθέμεθα	ἐτέθημεν
	2.	ἐθήκατε	ἔθεσθε	ἐτέθητε
	3.	ἔθηκαν	ἔθεντο	ἐτέθησαν

Subj. Sg. 1.   θῶ   θῶμαι   τεθῶ
       2.   θῇς   θῇ   τεθῇς
       3.   θῇ   θῆται   τεθῇ
       Pl. 1.   θῶμεν   θώμεθα   τεθῶμεν
       2.   θῆτε   θῆσθε   τεθῆτε
       3.   θῶσι(ν)   θῶνται   τεθῶσι(ν)

Impv. Sg. 2.   θές   θοῦ   τέθητι
       3.   θέτω   θέσθω   τεθήτω
       Pl. 2.   θέτε   θέσθε   τέθητε
       3.   θέντων or   θέσθων or   τεθέντων or
                   θέτωσαν   θέσθωσαν   τεθήτωσαν

Infin.   θεῖναι   θέσθαι   τεθῆναι

Part. Masc.   θείς   θέμενος   τεθείς
       Fem.   θεῖσα   θεμένη   τεθεῖσα
       Neut.   θέν   θέμενον   τεθέν

Ἵστημι

		Pres. Act.	**Pres. M./P.**	**Imperf. Act.**	**Imperf. M./P.**
Indic.	Sg. 1.	ἵστημι	ἵσταμαι	ἵστην	ἱστάμην
	2.	ἵστης	ἵστασαι	ἵστης	ἵστασο
	3.	ἵστησι(ν)	ἵσταται	ἵστη	ἵστατο
	Pl. 1.	ἵσταμεν	ἱστάμεθα	ἵσταμεν	ἱστάμεθα
	2.	ἵστατε	ἵστασθε	ἵστατε	ἵστασθε
	3.	ἱστᾶσι(ν)	ἵστανται	ἵστασαν	ἵσταντο

Subj.	Sg. 1.	ἱστῶ	ἱστῶμαι
	2.	ἱστῇς	ἱστῇ
	3.	ἱστῇ	ἱστῆται
	Pl. 1.	ἱστῶμεν	ἱστώμεθα
	2.	ἱστῆτε	ἱστῆσθε
	3.	ἱστῶσι(ν)	ἱστῶνται

Impv.	Sg. 2.	ἵστη	ἵστασο
	3.	ἱστάτω	ἱστάσθω
	Pl. 2.	ἵστατε	ἵστασθε
	3.	ἱστάντων or	ἱστάσθων or
		ἱστάτωσαν	ἱστάσθωσαν

| Infin. | | ἱστάναι | ἵστασθαι |

Part.	Masc.	ἱστάς	ἱστάμενος
	Fem.	ἱστᾶσα	ἱσταμένη
	Neut.	ἱστάν	ἱστάμενον

Besides first aorist forms, ἵστημι also has a second aorist active form, which is intransitive and means *I stood*.

		Aor. Act.	**2d Aor. Act.**	**Aor. Mid.**	**Aor. Pass.**
Indic.	Sg. 1.	ἔστησα	ἔστην	ἐστησάμην	ἐστάθην
	2.	ἔστησας	ἔστης	ἐστήσω	ἐστάθης
	3.	ἔστησε(ν)	ἔστη	ἐστήσατο	ἐστάθη
	Pl. 1.	ἐστήσαμεν	ἔστημεν	ἐστησάμεθα	ἐστάθημεν
	2.	ἐστήσατε	ἔστητε	ἐστήσασθε	ἐστάθητε
	3.	ἔστησαν	ἔστησαν	ἐστήσαντο	ἐστάθησαν
Subj.	Sg. 1.	στήσω	στῶ	στήσωμαι	σταθῶ
	2.	στήσῃς	στῇς	στήσῃ	σταθῇς
	3.	στήσῃ	στῇ	στήσηται	σταθῇ
	Pl. 1.	στήσωμεν	στῶμεν	στησώμεθα	σταθῶμεν
	2.	στήσητε	στῆτε	στήσησθε	σταθῆτε
	3.	στήσωσι(ν)	στῶσι(ν)	στήσωνται	σταθῶσι(ν)
Impv.	Sg. 2.	στῆσον	στῆθι	στῆσαι	στάθητι
	3.	στησάτω	στήτω	στησάσθω	σταθήτω
	Pl. 2.	στήσατε	στῆτε	στήσασθε	στάθητε
	3.	στησάντων or	στάντων or	στησάσθων or	σταθέντων or
		στησάτωσαν	στήτωσαν	στησάσθωσαν	σταθήτωσαν
Infin.		στῆσαι	στῆναι	στήσασθαι	σταθῆναι
Part.	Masc.	στήσας	στάς	στησάμενος	σταθείς
	Fem.	στήσασα	στᾶσα	στησαμένη	σταθεῖσα
	Neut.	στῆσαν	στάν	στησάμενον	σταθέν

Εἰμί

		Present	**Imperf.**	**Future**
Indic.	Sg. 1.	εἰμί	ἤμην	ἔσομαι
	2.	εἶ	ἦς	ἔσῃ

		3.	ἐστί(ν)	ἦν	ἔσται
	Pl.	1.	ἐσμέν	ἦμεν	ἐσόμεθα
		2.	ἐστέ	ἦτε	ἔσεσθε
		3.	εἰσί(ν)	ἦσαν	ἔσονται

Subj.	Sg.	1.	ὦ
		2.	ἦς
		3.	ἦ
	Pl.	1.	ὦμεν
		2.	ἦτε
		3.	ὦσι(ν)

Opt.	Sg.	1.	εἴην	ἐσοίμην
		2.	εἴης	ἔσοιο
		3.	εἴη	ἔσοιτο
	Pl.	1.	εἴημεν or εἶμεν	ἐσοίμεθα
		2.	εἴητε or εἶτε	ἔσοισθε
		3.	εἴησαν or εἶεν	ἔσοιντο

Impv.	Sg.	2.	ἴσθι
		3.	ἔστω
	Pl.	2.	ἔστε
		3.	ἔστων or
			ἔστωσαν

Infin.		εἶναι		ἔσεσθαι

Part.	Masc.	ὤν	ἐσόμενος
	Fem.	οὖσα	ἐσομένη
	Neut.	ὄν	ἐσόμενον

Appendix 2

Principal Parts of Selected Verbs

A parenthesis signifies that this principal part does not appear in the New Testament.

Present	Future	Aorist	Perf. Act.	Perf. M./P.	Aorist Pass.
ἀγαπάω *love*	ἀγαπήσω	ἠγάπησα	ἠγάπηκα	ἠγάπημαι	ἠγαπήθην
ἄγω *lead*	ἄξω	ἤγαγον/ἦξα	(ἦχα)	ἦγμαι	ἤχθην
αἴρω *take up*	ἀρῶ	ἦρα	ἦρκα	ἦρμαι	ἤρθην
ἀκούω *hear*	ἀκούσω	ἤκουσα	ἀκήκοα	(ἤκουσμαι)	ἠκούσθην
ἁμαρτάνω *sin*	ἁμαρτήσω	ἡμάρτησα /ἥμαρτον	ἡμάρτηκα	(ἡμάρτημαι)	(ἡμαρτήθην)
ἀφίημι *forgive*	ἀφήσω	ἀφῆκα	ἀφεῖκα	ἀφεῖμαι	ἀφέθην
βαίνω *go*	βήσομαι	ἔβην	βέβηκα	(βέβαμαι)	(ἐβάθην)
βάλλω *throw*	βαλῶ	ἔβαλον/ ἔβαλα	βέβληκα	βέβλημαι	ἐβλήθην
γίνομαι *become*	γενήσομαι	ἐγενόμην	γέγονα	γεγένημαι	ἐγενήθην
γινώσκω *know*	γνώσομαι	ἔγνων	ἔγνωκα	ἔγνωσμαι	ἐγνώσθην
γράφω *write*	γράψω	ἔγραψα	γέγραφα	γέγραμμαι	ἐγράφην
διδάσκω *teach*	διδάξω	ἐδίδαξα			ἐδιδάχθην
δίδωμι *give*	δώσω	ἔδωκα	δέδωκα	δέδομαι	ἐδόθην
δοξάζω *glorify*	δοξάσω	ἐδόξασα	(δεδόξακα)	δεδόξασμαι	ἐδοξάσθην
ἐγείρω *raise*	ἐγερῶ	ἤγειρα		ἐγήγερμαι	ἠγέρθην
ἐλπίζω *hope*	ἐλπιῶ	ἤλπισα	ἤλπικα		
ἔρχομαι *come*	ἐλεύσομαι	ἦλθον	ἐλήλυθα		

ἐσθίω *eat*	φάγομαι	ἔφαγον			
ἐτοιμάζω *prepare*	ἐτοιμάσω	ἡτοίμασα	ἡτοίμακα	ἡτοίμασμαι	ἡτοιμάσθην
εὑρίσκω *find*	εὑρήσω	εὗρον	εὕρηκα	(εὕρημαι)	εὑρέθην
ἔχω *have*	ἕξω	ἔσχον	ἔσχηκα		
θεραπεύω *heal*	θεραπεύσω	ἐθεράπευσα	(τεθεράπευκα)	τεθεράπευμαι	ἐθεραπεύθην
ἵστημι *stand*	στήσω	ἔστησα/ ἔστην	ἔστηκα	(ἕσταμαι)	ἐστάθην
καλέω *call*	καλέσω	ἐκάλεσα	κέκληκα	κέκλημαι	ἐκλήθην
κηρύσσω *preach*	κηρύξω	ἐκήρυξα	(κεκήρυχα)	(κεκήρυγμαι)	ἐκηρύχθην
κρίνω *judge*	κρινῶ	ἔκρινα	κέκρικα	κέκριμαι	ἐκρίθην
λαμβάνω *take*	λήμψομαι	ἔλαβον	εἴληφα	εἴλημμαι	ἐλήμφθην
λέγω *say*	ἐρῶ	εἶπον/εἶπα	εἴρηκα	εἴρημαι	ἐρρέθην/ ἐρρήθην
λείπω *leave*	λείψω	ἔλιπον	(λέλοιπα)	λέλειμμαι	ἐλείφθην
λύω *loose*	λύσω	ἔλυσα	(λέλυκα)	λέλυμαι	ἐλύθην
μένω *remain*	μενῶ	ἔμεινα	μεμένηκα		
ὁράω *see*	ὄψομαι	εἶδον	ἑόρακα/ ἑώρακα		ὤφθην
πάσχω *suffer*	(πείσομαι)	ἔπαθον	πέπονθα		
πείθω *persuade*	πείσω	ἔπεισα	πέποιθα	πέπεισμαι	ἐπείσθην
πέμπω *send*	πέμψω	ἔπεμψα	(πέπομφα)	(πέπεμμαι)	ἐπέμφθην
πιστεύω *believe*	(πιστεύσω)	ἐπίστευσα	πεπίστευκα	πεπίστευμαι	ἐπιστεύθην
ποιέω *do*	ποιήσω	ἐποίησα	πεποίηκα	πεποίημαι	(ἐποιήθην)
σῴζω *save*	σώσω	ἔσωσα	σέσωκα	σέσωσμαι/ σέσωμαι	ἐσώθην
τηρέω *keep*	τηρήσω	ἐτήρησα	τετήρηκα	τετήρημαι	ἐτηρήθην
τίθημι *place*	θήσω	ἔθηκα	τέθεικα	τέθειμαι	ἐτέθην
φιλέω *love*	(φιλήσω)	ἐφίλησα	πεφίληκα	(πεφίλημαι)	(ἐφιλήθην)

Summary of Topics

Grammar

Parts of Speech (chapter 1)
noun
  substantive
  stem
  ending
  case
    nominative case
    vocative case
    genitive case
    dative case
    accusative case
  gender
    masculine gender
    feminine gender
    neuter gender
    common gender
  declension
  number
    singular
    plural
    collective noun
    dual
adjective
  agreement
pronoun
  personal pronoun
  possessive pronoun
  reflexive pronoun
  reciprocal pronoun
  relative pronoun
  interrogative pronoun
  indefinite pronoun
  demonstrative pronoun
verb
  finite verb
    suffix
    prefix
    infix
    person

    first person
    second person
    third person
  tense
  aspect
  voice
    active voice
    middle voice
    passive voice
  mood
    indicative mood
    subjunctive mood
    optative mood
    imperative mood
  infinitive
adverb
participle
preposition
conjunction
particle
  interjection
morphology
The Sentence (chapter 2)
sentence
syntax
subject
  simple subject
  complete subject
predicate
  simple predicate
  complete predicate
ellipsis
types of verbs
  transitive verb
  intransitive verb
  linking verb
  copulative verb
  verb of incomplete predication
modifier
complement
classes of sentences

classified by thought
  declarative sentence
  interrogative sentence
  imperative sentence
  exclamatory sentence
classified by structure
  simple sentence
    compound subject
    compound predicate
  compound sentence
  complex sentence
  compound-complex sentence
phrases
  noun phrase
  prepositional phrase
  verbal phrase
    verbals
clauses
  independent clause *or* main clause
  dependent clause *or* subordinate
     clause
  noun clause *or* substantive clause
  adjectival clause
  adverbial clause
    final clause
    temporal clause
    local clause
    causal clause
    result clause
    conditional clause
    concessive clause
    comparative clause

Noun System

Nouns (chapter 3)
  declension
    first declension
    second declension
    third declension
  case
    nominative
      subject nominative
      predicate nominative
      nominative of address
      nominative absolute
      hanging nominative
      nominative of appellation
    vocative
    genitive

genitive of possession
genitive of relationship
partitive genitive
subjective genitive
objective genitive
genitive absolute
genitive of direct object
genitive of material or contents
descriptive genitive
genitive of apposition
epexegetical genitive
genitive of comparison
genitive of time
genitive of measure
genitive of source
dative
  dative of indirect object
  instrumental dative
  locative dative
  dative of time
  dative of possession
  dative of direct object
  dative of reference
  dative of advantage or
    disadvantage
  dative of manner
  dative of association
  dative of agency
accusative
  accusative of direct object
  double accusative
  accusative of time
  adverbial accusative

Adjectives (chapter 4)
  adjectives
    attributive adjective
    predicate adjective
    substantival adjective
    adverbial adjective
  comparison of adjectives
    positive degree
    comparative degree
    superlative degree
     elative
  numerals
    cardinal
    ordinal
Pronouns (chapter 5)
  terms
    antecedent
    referent

pronouns
  personal pronoun
  possessive pronoun
  reflexive pronoun
  reciprocal pronoun
  relative pronoun
    indefinite relative pronoun
  interrogative pronoun
  indefinite pronoun
  demonstrative pronoun
Articles (chapter 6)
  terms
    articular
    arthrous
    anarthrous
  uses
    anaphoric
    generic
  special rules
    Colwell's Rule
    Granville Sharp Rule
Prepositions (chapter 7)
  preposition
  postposition
  prepositional phrase
  proper prepositions
  improper prepositions

Verb System

Finite Verbs (chapters 8 and 9)
  inflection
  person
    first person
    second person
    third person
  number
    concord
    constructio ad sensum
  voice
    active voice
      simple active
      causative active
    middle voice
      direct middle
      intensive middle
      reciprocal middle
    passive voice
      simple passive
      permissive passive

agent
  primary agency *or* personal
    agency
  secondary agency *or* intermediate
    agency
  instrumental agency *or* imper-
    sonal agency
deponent verbs
aspect
  aoristic aspect
  imperfective aspect
  perfective aspect
mood
  indicative mood (mood of reality)
    declarative indicative
    imperatival indicative
    interrogative indicative
    subjunctive mood (mood
        of probability)
    hortatory subjunctive
    subjunctive of prohibition
    deliberative subjunctive
    subjunctive of emphatic negation
    final subjunctive
    content subjunctive
  optative mood (mood of possibility)
    voluntative optative
    potential optative
    imperative mood (mood
        of volition/intention)
    imperative of command
    imperative of prohibition
    imperative of entreaty
    imperative of permission
time (tense)
  aorist tense
    ingressive aorist
    effective aorist
    constative aorist
    gnomic aorist
    epistolary aorist
    dramatic aorist
  imperfect tense
    progressive imperfect
    iterative imperfect
    tendential imperfect
    inceptive imperfect
  pluperfect tense
  present tense
    descriptive present
    progressive present
    iterative present

tendential present
historical present
futuristic present
aoristic present
perfect tense
  intensive perfect
  consummative perfect
  dramatic perfect
future tense
  predictive future
  progressive future
  imperatival future
  deliberative future
future perfect tense
periphrastic tenses
  periphrastic imperfect
  periphrastic pluperfect
  periphrastic perfect
principal parts
  1. present active
  2. future active
  3. aorist active
  4. perfect active
  5. perfect middle/passive
  6. aorist passive
Infinitives (chapter 10)
complementary infinitive
epexegetical infinitive
infinitive of indirect discourse
substantival infinitive
infinitive of time
infinitive of purpose
infinitive of result
causal infinitive
imperatival infinitive
infinitive of indirect discourse
Participles (chapter 11)
adjectival participle
adverbial participle
  temporal participle
  causal participle
  telic/final participle
  conditional participle
  concessive participle
  instrumental participle
  complementary participle
  imperatival participle

  periphrastic participle
  participle of attendant circumstance
  participle absolute *or* genitive
    absolute
Adverbs (chapter 12)
adverb of time
adverb of manner
adverb of place
interrogative adverb
numerical adverb
adverb of degree
Conjunctions (chapter 12)
terms
  postpositive
  asyndeton
coordinating/paratactic conjunction
  copulative conjunction
  adversative conjunction
    eliminative adversative
    balancing adversative
  disjunctive conjunction
  inferential conjunction
  causal conjunction
subordinating/hypotactic conjunction
Particles (chapter 12)
negative particle
emphatic particle
Clauses (chapter 13)
temporal clause
relative clause
comparative clause
causal clause
local clause
purpose clause
result clause
content clause
conditional clause
  protasis
  apodosis
  first-class condition *or* simple
    condition
  second-class condition *or* contrary-
    to-fact condition
  third-class condition *or* more-
    probable future condition
  fourth-class condition *or* less-
    probable future condition

Subject Index

183

Greek Word Index

G reek words listed here are drawn from the grammatical and syntactical discussions. Greek words occurring in illustrative quotations from the New Testament can be found by using the Scripture index.

Scripture Index

David Alan Black (D.Theol., University of Basel, Switzerland) is professor of New Testament and Greek at Southeastern Baptist Theological Seminary and New Testament editor of the International Standard Version of the Bible. He has authored or edited twelve books. Dr. Black is also an avid horseman and student of Civil War history, participating in battle reenactments throughout the country.